Empire, Colony, Postcolony

Empire, Colony, Postcolony

Robert J. C. Young

WILEY Blackwell

This edition first published 2015
© 2015 Robert J. C. Young

Registered Office
John Wiley & Sons, Ltd, The Atrium, Southern Gate, Chichester, West Sussex, PO19 8SQ, UK

Editorial Offices
350 Main Street, Malden, MA 02148-5020, USA
9600 Garsington Road, Oxford, OX4 2DQ, UK
The Atrium, Southern Gate, Chichester, West Sussex, PO19 8SQ, UK

For details of our global editorial offices, for customer services, and for information about how to apply for permission to reuse the copyright material in this book please see our website at www.wiley.com/wiley-blackwell.

Library of Congress Cataloging-in-Publication Data
Young, Robert, 1950–
  Empire, colony, postcolony / Robert J. C. Young.
    pages cm
  Summary: "The first book to introduce the main historical and cultural parameters of the different categories of empire, colony, and postcolony, and the ways in which they are analysed today"– Provided by publisher.
  Includes bibliographical references and index.
  ISBN 978-1-4051-9340-5 (hardback) – ISBN 978-1-4051-9355-9 (paper) 1. Colonies. 2. Imperialism. 3. Post-colonialism. I. Title.
  JV105.Y68 2015
  325′.3–dc23
                    2015004134

A catalogue record for this book is available from the British Library.

Cover image: Palestinian youths practising parkour, southern Gaza strip. © Mohammed Salem / Reuters / Corbis

Set in 11/14pt Minion by SPi Global, Pondicherry, India
Printed and bound in Malaysia by Vivar Printing Sdn Bhd

1   2015

For Ann

dearest companion and friend
through generations

Contents

Acknowledgments

I would like to begin by thanking Emma Bennett, for suggesting to me that I should write a short book that would develop some of the conceptual and historical categories first presented in my *Postcolonialism: An Historical Introduction* (Wiley-Blackwell 2001). The present volume is intended to complement, develop, and update that earlier account in a different form; the reader who is interested in more specific and detailed histories of the anticolonial movements in the Soviet Union, South America, Africa, and Asia will find extended analyses of them there. In general, given the intended length of this book, and against the academic's natural impulse to give a long list of relevant sources, I have tried to keep references to a reasonable minimum. Although this book is designed to be read as a book, that is, in sequence, the individual chapters have also been designed to be relatively free standing; this necessarily requires occasional small repetitions.

At Wiley-Blackwell I would also like to thank Bridget Jennings and Ben Thatcher, and especially my former editor, the ever genial Andrew McNeillie.

I have been very fortunate in having a number of expert readers for the manuscript of this book at various stages. Stephen Howe read a late version with his customary attention to detail and dazzling encyclopedic historical knowledge, offering a host of useful suggestions and corrections. Douglas Kerr responded with characteristic elegance that made me consider unthought possibilities, rethink some knotty problems, and attend to my grammar; Hélène Quiniou read the manuscript with a Francophone philosophical brilliance that opened up a range of new possibilities, some of which must be held over for the future. Rita Kothari grappled with an early draft and asked some simple but characteristically penetrating questions about it; Mélanie Heydari read through a late version and pointed me towards many detailed improvements. I am sincerely grateful to them all and hope they feel that the final version is worth their very generous efforts. Virginia Smithson of the British Museum kindly located the Asante Ewer for me. I owe special thanks to Omar Mahdawi for walking me through Shatila Camp in West Beirut.

I would like to express my gratitude to New York University for supporting my research; Christopher Cannon for being such a considerate head of department; my colleagues on the Postcolonial Studies Project at NYU Toral Gajarawala and Jini Kim Watson; and also for collegiate discussions of all kinds, my colleagues John Archer, Tom Augst, Jennifer Baker, Una Chaudhuri, Patricia Crain, Patrick Deer, Carolyn Dinshaw, Juliet Fleming, Elaine Freedgood, Ernest Gilman, Lisa Gitelman, John Guillory, Richard Halpern, Phillip Harper, Josephine Hendin, David Hoover, Julia Jarcho, Wendy Lee, Larry Lockridge, John Maynard, Paula McDowell, Elizabeth McHenry, Maureen Mclane, Perry Meisel, Haruko Momma, Peter Nichols, Crystal A. Parikh, Mary Poovey, Sonya Posmentier, Catherine Robson, Martha Rust, Sukhdev Sandhu, Lytle Shaw, Jeff Spear, Gabrielle Star, Gregory Vargo, and John Waters. An especially big thank you to our administrators Lissette Florez, Susan McKeon, Taeesha Muhammad, Patricia Okoh-Esene, and Shanna Williams. My assistant, Hannah May Jocelyn, has helped to put me and my house in order, for which I remain very grateful. In Comparative Literature and elsewhere at NYU, many thanks too to Arjun Appadurai, Emily Apter, Lauren Benton, J. Michael Dash, Ana Maria Dopico, Allen Feldman, Dick Foley, Jay Garcia, Gayatri Gopinath, Hala Halim, Ben Kafka, Jacques Lezra, David Ludden, Nicholas Mirzoeff, Mary Louise Pratt, Arvind Rajagopal, Mark Sanders, Ella Shohat, Richard Sieburth, Robert Stam, Kate Stimpson, Jack Tchen, and Jane Tylus, and in New York more generally, Meena Alexander, Kate Ballen, Akeel Bilgrami, Tanya Fernando, Simon Gikandi, Kyoo Lee, Arwa Mahdawi, Rosalind Morris, Nick Nesbitt, Bruce Robbins, Mariam Said, Gayatri Spivak, Megan Vaughan, Tony Vidler, and Michael Wood. My thanks also to my students and graduate students over the past few years, particularly Shifa Ali, Durba Basu, Suzy Cater, Keren Dotan, Mosarrap Khan, Laurie

Lambert, Jo Livingstone, Nick Matlin, Rajiv Menon, Omar Miranda, Joe Napolitano, Adam Spanos, Alice Speri, David Sugarman, and Shirley Lau Wong. At NYU Abu Dhabi I have been fortunate to have many productive conversations with colleagues, particularly Awam Ampka, Alide Cagidemetrio, Walter Feldman, Ama Francis, Wail Hassan, Stephanie Hilger, Paulo Horta, Dale Hudson, Philip Kennedy, Masha Kirasirova, Martin Klimke, Sheetal Majithia, Judy Miller, Cyrus Patell, Maurice Pomerantz, Gunja Sengupta, Werner Sollors, Bryan Waterman, Katherine Williams, Shamoon Zamir; many thanks too to Hilary Ballon, Al Bloom, and Fabio Piano, for making it all possible.

I have learnt much from colleagues and contributors while editing *Interventions: International Journal of Postcolonial Studies*, particularly my fellow editors Neelam Srivastava and Teju Olaniyan, Sahar Sobhi Abdel-Hakim, and Stuti Khanna, as well as my patient assistants over the years Adrienne Ghaly, Weishun Lu, Kerrie Yang, and Heather Zuber. Many thanks too to our production editor Ben Wilcox, and Adam Burbage, our Managing Editor at T&F. I owe special thanks to Jack Messenger, our excellent, ever watchful copyeditor over many years, and also for this book.

My former colleagues at Wadham College, Oxford, have continued to provide inspiration and sustenance. I am always grateful to the College, and in particular to Terry Eagleton, Robin Fiddian, John Gurney, Stephen Heyworth, Christina Howells, Colin Mayer, Ankhi Mukherjee, Bernard O'Donoghue, Reza Sheikholeslami, and Oren Sussman, and elsewhere at Oxford, Elleke Boehmer, David Bradshaw, Maria Donapetry, Vincent Gillespie, Dhana Hughes, Sue Jones, David Keen, Hermione Lee, Laura Marcus, Peter McDonald, Heather O'Donoghue, William Outhwaite, Sowon Park, and the late Jon Stallworthy.

In talks and travel in many countries, including my own, I have been lucky to enjoy extended, hospitable conversations with many friends and colleagues over the years, particularly Marian Aguiar, Mai Al Nakib, Corina Angel, Isobel and Michael Armstrong, Derek Attridge, Deepika Bahri, Etienne Balibar, Emilienne Baneth-Nouailhetas, Cristina Baptista, Geoffrey Bennington, Omar Berrada, Homi K. Bhabha, Rosa Braidotti, Nadia Butt, Dipesh Chakravorty, Amit and Rosinka Chaudhuri, Caterina Colomba, Leyla Dakhli, David Damrosch, Theo d'Haen, Arif Dirlik, Maria Renata Dolce, PrathimMaya Dora-Laskey,

Tobias Döring, Maud Ellmann, Rita Felski, Farah Ghaderi, Luke Gibbons, Paul Gilroy, Lucy Graham, Sabry Hafez, Stephen Heath, Diana Hinds, Elaine Ho, Habib Imtiaz, Maher Jarrar, Claire Joubert, Tom Keenan, Jean Khalfa, Dirk Klopper, Abhijit Kothari, Fran Kral, David Lloyd, Chandani Lokuge, Cristina Lombardi-Diop, Paul Lowndes, Jo MacDonagh, Elissa Marder, Susan Matthews, Achille Mbembe, Matthew Meadows, Ana Mendes, Ranjini Mendis, Aamir Mufti, Susanne Mühleisen, Francis Mulrea, Parvati Nair, Esmail Nashif, Siri Nergaard, Lynda Ng, Sarah Nuttall, Annalisa Oboe, Sandra Ponzanesi, Chris Prentice, Ato Quayson, Ruvani Ranasinha, Jacqueline Rose, Nicholas Royle, Sara Salih, Abdelahad Sebti, Rumina Sethi, Mark Stein, Stephanos Stephanides, Robert Stockhammer, Weimin Tang, Harish Trivedi, Vron Ware, John Wilkinson, Clair Wills, and Thanos Zartaloudis: I warmly thank them all.

My family, as always, has been my best resource: Ann, to whom this book is dedicated, Elizabeth, my companion through all my years, Amtul, who is ever hospitable and generous, my wonderful and always loving Maryam, Yasmine, and Isaac, and my dearest Badral.

A small amount of material in chapters 3 and 5 draws on my article "Colónia and Imperium" in Barbara Cassin's *Dictionary of Untranslatables*, trans. Emily Apter et al. (Princeton: Princeton University Press, 2014). The citation from *The Little Prince* in the final chapter is also invoked in my article "What is the Postcolonial?," *Ariel* 40: 1 (2009) 18–19.

1

Introduction

Men make their own history, but they do not make it as they please;
they do not make it under self-selected circumstances, but under
circumstances existing already, given and transmitted from the past.
The tradition of all dead generations weighs like a nightmare on the
brains of the living. (Karl Marx, The Eighteenth Brumaire of Louis
Bonaparte, *1852)*

I

In an era of globalization, why should we care anymore about empires
or colonies? Have not times moved on? Why should anyone be bothered
with the history of fifty or more years ago when the world has changed
so dramatically? Why carp on about the past when the Chinese and
Indian economies are expanding exponentially and altering the economic
and political landscape? Have not neoliberal economics totally transformed the global political scene? Surely progress and a desire for the
new, not the presence of the past, are the constant state of things?

   Or are things really so different? Has the history of the world had so
little to do with the way that we live today? Are forced labor and slavery
really just history? Do the many wars and civil wars of the twenty-first
century, the civil strife and unrest, the ubiquitous presence of terrorism,

Empire, Colony, Postcolony, First Edition. Robert J. C. Young.
© 2015 Robert J. C. Young. Published 2015 by John Wiley & Sons, Ltd.

exist only in the present, with no relation to the past? Do the problems of the West or of the global South have nothing to do with the very formation of the nations that are identified with those opposing terms? Have neoliberal economics merely perpetuated a new form of empire that has moved into a different phase?

There are many ways of understanding the world and the complexities of our present. One way is to examine how we are living out our lives in part as the product of our past. To fathom the many issues and conflicts that today seem to pose almost insurmountable problems – terrorism, fundamentalism, wars in Africa and the Middle East, insurgency in India, Sri Lanka, or Thailand – it helps to understand where those problems have come from and under what conditions they have emerged. Sometimes it can even help to guide our political judgments: with their knowledge of what had happened before, few historians would have advocated the invasion of Afghanistan in 2001. As the Spanish philosopher George Santayana famously put it: "those who cannot remember the past, are condemned to repeat it."

 Some things continue in other forms. Colonialism and imperialism involved the subjection of one people by another, and developed in their modern varieties in conjunction with other kinds of domination: of women, of slaves, of minorities, of the poor, of relatively powerless sov- ereign peoples, of the resources of the earth. So long as oppressive power of that kind continues, then analysis of the forms and practices of colonialism and imperialism remains relevant to the problems that we face today.

II

Order something on the Internet and you soon come to the moment of entering your address. At this point you will often be presented with a drop-down box that contains a predefined list of the names of all countries, starting with Afghanistan and ending with Zimbabwe. The list is almost two hundred and fifty countries long. Suddenly, your country is put on an equal footing with all others: you may live in one of the western countries which took part in the invasion of Afghanistan in 2001, but here Afghanistan sits proudly at the top of the list, and you will have to scroll down almost the whole way to the bottom to find the United Kingdom or the United States. We take it for granted that everyone lives in or comes from a particular country, and that the world is made up of diverse, separate nations that are all represented in the organization called the United Nations, which oversees the governance of the world.[1]

Open Bartholomew's *The Century Atlas of the World*, published in London in 1902, and you will find a list of "Principal States with their Colonies and Protectorates." The number of such states here amounts to only thirty-seven. What happened, then, between 1902 and today? Not only are there fewer countries – neither Afghanistan nor Zimbabwe are to be found – but the names are also different. Here the names are not listed alphabetically, as on the Internet drop-down box, but by the size of the territory that they designate:

1 British Empire
2 Russian Empire
3 Chinese Empire (including Korea)
4 France
5 United States (including Hawaii, Cuba, Porto Rico [*sic*], the Philippines, Guam, and Tutuila, &c)
6 Brazil
7 Argentine Republic
8 Ottoman Empire
9 German Empire
10 Congo Free State
11 Portugal
12 Netherlands
13 Mexico
14 Peru
15 Persia
16 Bolivia
17 Columbia
18 Venezuela
19 Morocco
20 Sweden and Norway
21 Chili [*sic*]
22 Italy

23   Siam
24   Austria-Hungary
25   Abyssinia
26   Spain
27   Central America (5 states)
28   Japan
29   Ecuador
30   Denmark
31   Paraguay
32   Rumania
33   Bulgaria and E. Rumella (included in Ottoman Empire)
34   Greece
35   Servia [*sic*]
36   Switzerland
37   Belgium

It's an interesting list. Several countries that existed at that time, such as Liberia, are not even mentioned. Apart from the ranking by territorial size, what distinguishes it from a modern list is that some states are described as empires (if so, it now seems strange that France, Austria-Hungary, or Japan were not described as empires at that time). Portugal and Spain were no longer considered empires, though they had been empires and still had colonies; Denmark and Belgium if not empires certainly had colonies. Technically, the Congo Free State at that time was an independent fiefdom of the Belgian King: it would be assimilated into the Belgian Empire as a colony in 1908 after the scandalous conditions there were exposed. Morocco, whose coastal territories were already (and still are, under a different name) a Spanish "protectorate," would be divided up by France and Spain two years later in 1904.

Many of the countries on the list had been part of other empires over the previous one hundred and fifty years: Belgium itself, Italy, Greece, Serbia, Romania, the United States, Mexico, Argentina, Brazil, Peru, Bolivia, Columbia, Venezuela, Chile, Central America, Ecuador, Paraguay. Even Switzerland had been occupied by the French between 1798 and 1815. In fact very few of the countries had not been colonies of some kind in modern times: some that were themselves empires – Britain, China, France, Russia, Turkey – plus Abyssinia, Japan, Persia,

Siam. Abyssinia was then invaded and occupied by Italy in 1936; Persia (Iran) was occupied by the British and Russians in 1941; Japan was occupied by the United States in 1945. Thailand was the only country that managed to avoid colonization, even by the Japanese, though like China and Japan itself in the nineteenth century, it was obliged to grant extraterritorial "concessions" and is often described in the period as a "semi-colony." Though repeated attempts have been made to conquer Afghanistan since the nineteenth century, it has never been successfully colonized, apart from brief periods in which the colonizers rarely if ever controlled the whole country; in earlier times, it did, however, form part of the Persian Achaemenid, Sassanid, and Safavid empires. China which was already conceding territories to the imperial powers in the nineteenth century (by World War I, ten of the world's most powerful countries had concessions in China) was then invaded and partially colonized by the Japanese in the twentieth century. France was occupied by Germany; Russia underwent a convulsive revolution which prompted the international twelve-nation alliance invasion of 1917, followed by the German invasion of 1941, defeated at the cost of millions of lives. Turkey, which the Allied powers tried to dismember almost entirely in 1923, managed to hold them off enough to create its modern boundaries. During the period from 1750 to 2000 only Britain, Russia, Thailand, and Turkey have remained autonomous states throughout, albeit in changing geographical and political configurations. This autonomy has not preserved them from invasion, sequestration of their territory, internal revolution, or separatist campaigns. All these countries face movements demanding independence or political autonomy – from Scotland, Chechnya, the Malay Pattani, and Kurdistan.

We perhaps think of the world as it is as permanent, but it is chastening to reflect that in the last two hundred and fifty years, scarcely more than a breath in human history, its political stability has been minimal. Go back a few more hundred years, and the story hardly becomes more encouraging. State formations, whether as empires, nations, or unions, come and go, across the Americas, Europe, the Middle East, Africa, and Asia. From a longer perspective, the history of the world amounts to the formation and reformation of empires, appearing, expanding, and contracting like biological forms constantly emerging, growing, usurping, transforming, overpowering, retreating, disintegrating.

Historically most empires gave way to further empires. The end of the European empires, by contrast, produced a new global political formation that distinguishes them from all empires that preceded them: the world of nation-states. It was in that environment that the postcolonial emerged as a specific way of addressing the inequities and injustices of both imperial rule and its global aftermath. As V. S. Naipaul put it in 1967: "The empires of our times were short-lived, but they have altered the world forever; their passing away is their least significant feature" (Naipaul 1967: 38).

Note

1   Yet at the United Nations only 192 countries are represented. Where do the additional fifty or so names in our address list come from? Some of them are uninhabited, such as Bouvet Island, in the Antarctic, a colony of Norway. Others have names such as "Palestinian Territories, Occupied," "United States Minor Outlying Islands," "Netherland Antilles," or "British Virgin Islands." None of these addresses or destinations is a sovereign country.

2

Empire

"My name is Ozymandias, King of Kings:
Look on my works, ye mighty, and despair!"
Nothing beside remains. Round the decay
Of that colossal wreck, boundless and bare,
The lone and level sands stretch far away.
(Percy Bysshe Shelley,
"Ozymandias," 1818)

Considered from a historical perspective, what is most extraordinary about empires is the constant metamorphosis intrinsic to their very existence, their rise and fall, formation, reformation, and deformation. Every empire changed the culture of the territory under its rule, but that transformation would in turn give way to another. Despite their grandiosity, power, and claims of endurance, empires have historically been unstable, their boundaries constantly altering through the course of their existence like the protean shifting outlines of living amoeba. Empires in fact can only be charted properly with varying or animated maps – in general they were modified so frequently that any map can only be a snapshot of an empire's extent at any particular moment. Against this constant transformation of boundaries, and pattern of rise, fall, and extinction, the reiterated ideology of empires has been one of stability and endurance, a paradox highlighted with reverberating irony in Shelley's famous poem "Ozymandias" about the Egyptian pharaoh better

Empire, Colony, Postcolony, First Edition. Robert J. C. Young.
© 2015 Robert J. C. Young. Published 2015 by John Wiley & Sons, Ltd.

known as Ramesses II. At the end of the poem, Shelley cites the grand imperial claim made in the statue's inscription on its base, but centuries later its wrecked state, its location in the middle of the empty desert, works to ironize and completely reverse its original intended meaning.

always on the attack & defense

As any empire expanded, so did the extent of its boundaries: on the one hand this only prompted the desire for further conquests, while on the other hand it made those peripheries harder and harder to defend, more open to attack. Every new conquest or annexation produces more borders to secure, and further limits against which to push and which territory to conquer. At any sign of weakness, those already conquered might take their chance to rebel. Meanwhile, far distant frontiers become less and less determinate the further away they are, and imperial authority grows ever more tenuous at those points. This principle forms the inherent vulnerability of all empires, and one reason why most of them remained unstable and eventually collapsed. Empires have almost always been destroyed by competition for power from without or from within. The story of empire is consistently one of expansion, usurpation, contraction, and dissolution.

spread too thin

Many empires have been driven by ambition and the aspiration for empire of individual conquerors like Ozymandias (Ramesses II c.1303–1213 BCE)—such as Cyrus the Great (576–530 BCE)—Alexander (356–323 BCE)—Julius Caesar (100–44 BCE)—Timur (Tamerlane) (1336–1405)—Genghis Khan (1162–1227)—Napoleon Bonaparte (1769–1821), and Hitler (1889–1945), or developed by a series of such figures, as in the case of the Ottoman Empire (Murad II, Mehmed II, Selim I, Suleiman the Magnificent). Some empires, such as the British, expanded, contracted, expanded, and contracted again more episodically without being driven by a particular sovereign ruler (in the nineteenth century the historian John Seeley famously claimed that the British Empire had been acquired in a "fit of absence of mind") (Seeley 1971: 33). Nevertheless the motivations for empire, whether of sovereign, trader, or explorer, have usually been similar: glory, power, and money. As Jane Burbank and Frederick Cooper put it in their *Empires in World History*: "The men who sailed forth from Western Europe across the seas in the fifteenth and sixteenth centuries did not set out to create 'merchant empires' or 'western colonialism.' They sought wealth outside

goals of empire

the confines of a continent where large-scale ambitions were constrained by tensions between lords and monarchs, religious conflicts, and the Ottomans' lock on the Eastern Mediterranean" (Burbank and Cooper 2010: 149). These explorers were the entrepreneurs of their time, trying to bypass the constrictions of class and rank in their own societies. Most empires have been driven by the desire for wealth extracted from somewhere else: Julius Caesar invaded Britain for the same reason the Spanish invaded the Americas: gold. The other motivation has been religion: whether for religious freedom (the Pilgrim Fathers), or more often for religious proselytization. In allocating the division of the Americas between the Spanish and the Portuguese, the Pope, as God's representative on earth, had justified their colonization on the grounds of the promise of the conversion of the indigenous peoples to Christianity, in an era when Catholic missionaries such as Francis Xavier were also moving into Africa and the East. The Islamic Caliphate expanded from Saudi Arabia from the time of the Prophet Mohammed; in accordance with the Constitution of Medina, religious tolerance for "the people of the book" (Jews, Christians) was the normative rule, even if in practice it was not always observed, particularly with respect to Sunni–Shi'a relations, and there were certainly missions that produced, or enforced, large-scale conversions.

Many European empires were also created in part through the drive for emigration and settlement producing settler colonies on the original Greek model, in order to get rid of surplus, unemployed and unproductive populations: the Spanish in the Americas, the Dutch in South Africa, the English in North America and Australasia, the Italians in Libya – just as today the hungry, the unemployed, or the underpaid of the world migrate in search of a better life. The settlement colonies where such people landed, far from the metropolitan center, have always been prone to detach themselves from the empire, particularly if they were an ocean or two away.

However diverse their political formation, all empires have been geographically extensive: for an empire to be worthy of its name, its boundaries must be far-reaching. To call your territory an empire when it is the size of a city, state, or a province merely suggests unrealistic aspiration – no one quite seems to know why New York calls itself "the Empire State."[1] Traditionally, empires were political formations that were developed over time from particular geographical areas or through nomadic occupation. For the most part, they grew by con-quest, though sometimes by dynastic marriage. Most empires have existed simultaneously with others, along with local kingdoms, states, or nomadic tribal groups that lived outside any imperial umbrella. To the extent that empires trace extensive and sometimes enduring political formations, they offer ways of constructing large-scale histor-ical narratives on a global scale. Today, globalization has meant that historians often present world history as the history of its empires. That is one way of organizing it, a return in fact to the perspective of the eighteenth century when Enlightenment historians such as Gibbon or Volnay were preoccupied with the decline and fall of empires. During the nineteenth century's age of imperialism, with its attendant racial and cultural hierarchies, attention switched to a focus on civili-zations. In the twentieth century, traditional history in western coun-tries preferred to employ the narrative of the expansion of Europe, beginning with the history of "Ancient" civilizations by which was meant Greece and Rome, moving on to the development of European culture during the Renaissance, the flowering of modernity with the Enlightenment in the eighteenth century, the expansion of Europe and the formation of European empires, followed by the world wars, the Cold War, decolonization, and the advent of a world of nation-states. All this could be presented implicitly or explicitly as part of a larger narrative, of the progress of (western) "civilization," often identified with "modernity," as such.

Empire and Civilization

What is the difference between an empire and a civilization? Very little in practice, for many are identified as both. Some "civilizations" of course did not aspire to the status of empire, but they probably did not call themselves a "civilization" either. That is what we call them now because we classify them as societies that produced their own distinct forms of settlement, agriculture, technology, trade, writing, religion, and art, all things that are also often characteristics of empires. The choice of term depends more on whether you wish to foreground the cultural or the political category. We speak of the early Indus Valley Harappan civilization only because it is so early that we have little detailed information about its political organization – even its duration is a matter of debate. As a cultural category, though civilization has always been in the eye of the beholder, it has usually been identified with the development of cities and their urban culture (the word itself derives from *civis*, citizen). Civilization has typically been opposed to foreign societies regarded as uncivilized, "barbarian," "savage," or "primitive." Many empires have claimed to be bringing civilization to the territories that they appropriated. One of the major justifications of empire in the nineteenth century was that westerners were fully civilized while non-westerners existed in varying states of non-civilization – imperialism therefore was claimed to bring "civilization" to them, an ideology most acutely formulated by the French in their concept of the *mission civilisatrice*, founded on their assumption that there was (or is) a *civilisation française*. Civilization in this instance functioned as a secular version, appropriate for a Republican state, of a much older justification of empire and colonization: Christian conversion. It was only the Spanish and the Portuguese who had been formally obliged to justify colonization and empire through missionary work, but all colonies were subjected to missionary endeavors, and missionaries utilized any available colonial outposts to facilitate their efforts, even at times urging further colonization on their behalf. Though in practice their relation with colonial administrators was often somewhat conflictual, the link between missionary work and colonization was a means of giving the practice of empire an aura of moral purpose. Civilization and missionary work on behalf of civilization's religion, Christianity, became almost identical in the mind of many imperialists, with both being regarded as a self-explanatory good, much like overseas "aid" and "development" in more recent times.

This imperial history has made the whole idea of "civilization" difficult to employ today, since the very concept is widely recognized to involve many ethnocentric cultural assumptions. As a result, historians now prefer to use the term "empire," which suggests a more comparative, historical, less judgmental perspective. If the two are often still identified, it remains the case that some empires have produced more "civilization," in the sense of more distinctive and enduring

def. of civilization

(margin annotation: → b/c they lasted such a long time)

cultures, than others. Those that lasted longest, such as that of Egypt, had the best chance of creating a civilization of their own. Egypt, unusually, was comparatively uninterested in spreading its own culture abroad; most empires, by contrast, have tried to impose some mark of the imperial realm on the territories that fell under imperial sway: a common sovereign, followed by a common language, script, law, coinage, architectural style, and, sometimes, religion. In this respect, the first major "empires" were generally also distinct civilizations – Egypt, Assyria, Babylon. At its greatest extent, in the fifteenth century BCE, the boundaries of the Egyptian Empire extended as far as modern Turkey in the North, and Eritrea in the South, but despite its size it was only one of the great powers of its day, coexisting in the territory of what is now called the Middle East with many rival empires, such as the Babylonian and Assyrian. Subsequent empires in Asia included the Achaemenid or Persian Empire under Cyrus the Great, the Macedonian Empire under Alexander the Great (which stretched to the Himalayas), and the various dynastic Chinese empires whose geographical borders habitually shifted. Empires on the Indian subcontinent changed many times between the time of Alexander and the arrival of the Mughals. The history of the Indian subcontinent has been the constant creation, dissolution, and reconfiguration of multiple empires, of varying geographical extent, the largest of which included the Mauryan Empire under Ashoka the Great, the British Indian Empire, the Buddhist Pala Empire, the Muslim Mughal Empire, and the Hindu Gupta Empire. Other major empires elsewhere before the modern period would include empires outside the Eurasian landmass such as those in Mali, and in Central (Aztec) and South (Inca) America, and, back on the Eurasian landmass, the Greek and the Roman, the second Persian Empire, followed by the religious empires of the Byzantine and Holy Roman Empires and the Abbasid Caliphate. By the seventeenth century the Ottoman Empire stretched from the Persian Gulf to Algiers to the borders of Vienna. The largest empire in terms of contiguous landmass in any period, however, was the Mongol Empire of the thirteenth to fourteenth centuries founded by Genghis Khan, which extended from the Pacific to Europe and is supposed to have included 30 percent of the world's population within its no doubt somewhat tenuous boundaries.

(margin annotations: tried to make them unified in a way; "Mongols" = lgest. empire)

The Geography of Empire: Land vs. Global Maritime Empires

Despite their differences, all these empires had one thing in common that enabled the transmission of their particular cultures or civilizations: they were made up of contiguous territories on a single landmass. The Islamic caliphates, for example, spread out wherever the undemanding dromedary camel could take the conquerors (Silverstein 2010: 6). Alexander the Great extended the eastern boundary of the Greek Empire into India, while founding the city of Alexandria in Egypt. Expansion over adjoining territory was also the basis of some modern empires, such as Napoleonic France, Nazi Germany, and the Russian (Soviet) Empire, all of which operated in the more traditional form of landmass expansionist empires. Russia, proclaimed an empire by Peter the Great in 1721, has consistently incorporated, or reincorporated, adjacent territories from the original Kievan Rus'. By 1866 it had moved overseas, or rather over ice, reaching from North America (with settlements in Alaska and California) to the Baring Sea, from the Arctic to the Baltic. Having given up much of its imperial territory during World War I, then regaining it after World War II, and then losing it again with the dissolution of the Soviet Union in 1991, by 2014 Russia had resumed its expansionist mode, annexing the Crimea and fermenting separatism in Eastern and Southern Ukraine – a development impressively forecast in 2001 by the political scientist and analyst of the structure and dynamics of empires, Alexander J. Motyl (Motyl 2001).

The United States in some sense operated as a mirror image of Russia. While Russia expanded ever eastwards, as soon as they achieved independence in 1776, American colonists started expanding westwards from the original thirteen colonies on the Eastern seaboard of North America into territory hitherto explicitly designated by the British as Native American reserves; in 1803 the United States contracted for the Louisiana Purchase from Napoleon and bought the remaining French territories in North America. An imperial policy was followed more deliberately under President Polk when the United States annexed Texas in 1845, leading to the Mexican–American War which in turn led to the incorporation of Arizona, California, Nevada, New Mexico, and Utah. Having reached the western limit of the Pacific Ocean, from 1845 the

United States began to acquire territories beyond its own immediate landmass, starting with a concession in China negotiated in the Treaty of Wang Hiya. Alaska was purchased from Russia in 1867. More controversially, Hawaii was incorporated in 1898 after Queen Lili'uokalani had been overthrown in 1893 (Hawaii remains the only US state whose flag contains the British Union Jack). At that point, the United States began to take the form of a maritime empire, absorbing overseas territories taken by military force. Yet the difficulties soon became apparent: only two of these, Alaska and the islands of Hawaii, have been made into a state of the union. Other territories, many of which were annexed at the time of the Spanish American War (1898) – Cuba, Puerto Rico, the Philippines, American Samoa, Northern Mariana islands, the Marshall islands – were either subsequently granted independence, became independent, or remain suspended in the curious status of "unincorporated territory." In 1913, with a change of president, the United States' sixty-year period of seeking to be a global empire in the Pacific was changed dramatically in favor of national self-determination for all colonies around the world. Empire and democracy have coexisted uneasily as US national policy ever since.

Before achieving independence, the United States itself had been a part of a very different kind of empire that was not formed on a single landmass but stretched around the world: the global maritime empire of Britain (Darwin 2013). This was the other form of empire, involving the occupation of landmass on far-away continents (Howe 2002). Such empires are best understood as global maritime empires, operating as transoceanic economies based on trading posts networked around the world and an aggregate of geographically dispersed colonies, all held together by the new technology of ocean-going ships and, later, undersea telegraph cables.

For the most part, earlier empires consisted of proximate territories across a single landmass. From the eighth to the eleventh centuries, however, the Vikings traveled extensively, in their extraordinary long ships which used an advanced technology that enabled them to sail against the wind as far as North America, Russia, and the Eastern Mediterranean, not only raiding as is well known from popular mythology, but also founding colonies in present day Newfoundland, Labrador, Greenland, Iceland, and even Southern Italy. While Vikings set up colonies, they were never agglomerated into a connected empire, in part because there was no stable state in the modern sense at home to be its center. By the early sixteenth century, Europeans were building ocean-going "caravels" that used navigational aids such as the astrolabe, compass, and cross-staff (technology in part derived from maritime Asia) that enabled sailors to return across the oceans. As a result, it became possible to form empires that were not geographically proximate. Unlike the Vikings, these later colonists were able to keep in touch with their homelands relatively easily, however distant they may have been.

This one factor distinguished modern European empires from all others that had preceded them. Combined with the development of other forms of military and communications technology, such as fire-arms and cannon (first used in China) (Goody 2012: 274), or later the machine gun and the telegraph, European states were able to control territories all over the world to which they had no geographical proximity. In this vast imperial web whose fundamental organizing principle was the flow of trade, three different kinds of colony can be distinguished: the settler colony, the unsettled exploitation colony, and the fort or naval base, which we may call the garrison colony.[2] In the modern era, the garrison colony has not comprised a city, as in Roman times, but a military base, such as the sovereign territories of Britain and the United States on the islands of Cyprus (Akrotiri and Dhekelia) and Cuba (Guantanamo), respectively, which are wholly military enclaves. The strangest case is Diego Garcia, which was sold to the United Kingdom by Mauritius while still a British colony in 1965; the British Labour government then forcibly resettled the Chagossian inhabitants in order to lease the island to the United States for use as a naval base; since 2001, it has operated as a site for extraordinary rendi-tion.[3] The island's former residents continue to campaign for their return home, despite losing their last legal case against the British government in 2008.

While oceanic economies made up of trading networks such as those of the Indian Ocean or Southeast Asia certainly existed in the past, globally dispersed maritime empires were an exclusively European entity until the advent of the Japanese Empire at the end of the nineteenth century. International trade in luxury commodities had been going on since at least Greek and Roman times, but in the sixteenth century the

Ottoman Empire's complete control of the Eastern Mediterranean cut off easy access to the traditional land routes. Europeans therefore took the elaborate route all the way around Africa to the East instead. European maritime empires began in 1402 with the development of Spanish and Portuguese empires in the Canary Islands and the Azores, North Africa, West Africa, Asia, and the Americas. While both the Spanish and Portuguese established trading posts along the coasts of Africa and throughout South and Southeast Asia, it was in the Americas that they developed the first European transoceanic land empire, initially through the Spanish conquest of two indigenous empires, the Aztec and the Inca. The complex history of European expansion in North America, with territories variously held by Spain, Portugal, France, Holland, and Britain, and of the acquisition of colonies in Africa and Asia, was accompanied by centuries of wars between European states. These became global in extent as the European powers vied with each other in the colonial sphere. The result was that the empires themselves were remarkably unstable, with territories frequently switching sovereignty: in later years, the concept of international law would be developed in order to stabilize rival imperial interests. At the same time, the influx of South American silver and gold gave a dramatic boost to European economies which were in the process of developing early industrial formations such as the plantation, while the transportation of millions of slaves from Africa to the Americas in order to work in mines and on plantations devastated the cultures of the African continent and created a social system based on race whose consequences remain with us today. So too with the effects on the indigenous peoples of the Americas, now thought to have numbered around fifty million before 1492, who were subjected to the deprivations of imported diseases, slavery, and simple genocide.

The last remaining state of the Inca Empire, Vilcabamba in Peru, was not conquered by the Spanish until 1572. Just over two hundred years later, the American colonies of the various empires of Britain, France, Spain, and Portugal began to reestablish independence, albeit in a rather different form, from 1776 to 1822, initiating the epoch of postcolonial states.[4] Even in the modern era, therefore, postcoloniality began nearly two hundred and fifty years ago. Then, as now, however, for indigenous people, national self-determination often led to worse treatment by local governments no longer overseen by imperial efforts to enforce equitable treatment for native peoples. The beginning of the postcolonial era also illustrates the fact that countries such as Russia, the United States, and China, which expanded as land empires that were integrated into the state, have sustained the geographical extent of their empires much more successfully than those European nations that developed global maritime empires – which have now almost disappeared.

The Governance of Empire

There have been many empires throughout human history, but it is the Roman Empire, developed from the concept of the *imperium* – that is, the supreme power of the ruler – that generally functions as the fundamental template for the conceptualization of empire. Empire is centered on the language of command, *imperāre*, on the rule of the emperor and the territories over which that rule extends (compare *translatio imperii*, the chronological succession of transfers of supreme power that form the basis of medieval and imperial histories). Empire therefore involves a territory, or territories, whose sovereign is an emperor, or someone fulfilling an equivalent function, who has supreme power. This need not take a form of absolute rule, but does assume supreme political dominion that extends to the boundaries of the empire. It has already been suggested that the drive for all imperial expansion almost always involves the desire for the acquisition of wealth, power, and prestige by means of conquest. But once an empire has been established, how can it be governed? The vast geographic expanse of empires made communication and control – in the days before planes, railways, and telephones, even a postal service – almost unimaginable for us today. To read contemporary newspapers in Britain published in 1857 is to realize that the East India Company and government in London had almost no idea of what was happening in India at that time aside from the reports that would arrive episodically on returning ships, giving descriptions of events months after they had taken place. Governance had to be adapted to the vast distances and elongated time of empire, as well as being woven closely with the economic exploitation that formed its rationale.

While some empires such as the Ottomans utilized a system in which relatively independent local lords or rulers acknowledged the sovereignty of the emperor or sultan, others such as the Spanish were divided into provinces and run by viceroys or governors responsible to the King or sovereign presiding at the center. Some, such as the British Empire in India, used a combination of both. The key to governance was the production of revenue: here the tribute was the most common fiscal arrangement since it could be used in situations of direct or indirect rule. As in Spanish America, conquest enforced a relation of subservience that ensured regular payment of tributes by local leaders (who would, in turn, raise the money through further tributes, taxes on land rents, or commodities such as salt). In utilizing the tribute structure, the Spanish were in fact merely following the same informal arrangements that had been used in the Aztec Empire. The Ottoman empires and the British in India also used this traditional system: contrary to perceptions in the nineteenth century, in certain respects as empires they were in fact very similar. In order to extract wealth in the form of exportable commodities, whether silver, gold, or sugar, many empires – the Incas, the Spanish and Portuguese, the British, the French, the German, the Japanese – resorted to the use of various kinds of forced labor. In economic terms, early empires with their slave mines and plantations operated on a strictly mercantilist basis, with tight commercial regulations under which typically the commodities produced could only be sold to the "home" country.

The major alternative to the traditional systems of governance was developed by the Chinese: a centralized form of central government and state bureaucracy, but with a semi-autonomous provincial administration, first developed in the second century BCE. The Chinese Empire was run through a bureaucracy, with administrators who were selected through a competitive imperial examination. The arrangement was adapted centuries later, in various forms and with varying success, by European imperial powers including Britain and France. Appointing administrators by ability rather than connections was one key element; putting them into an administrative service with clearly defined ranks and therefore a career ladder which they could ascend, meant that imperial administrators tended to develop a loyalty to the system which they served. This helped to hold the vast machinery of the empire together.

companies use this but why not government officials? (handwritten annotation)

Among European empires, trained administrators would be moved from country to country to prevent them becoming too involved with particular localities (corporations use the same technique today with their employees, who, as with their imperial forbears, are left with no loyalties except to the company, or so it is hoped).

In practice, most empires used a variety of means of governance that developed pragmatically. In the case of Britain, for example, some territories would be assimilated into the country itself (Wales 1535, Scotland 1707, Ireland 1801), while all other colonies were kept distinct as overseas possessions of one kind or another (colonies, dominions, mandates, protectorates, and other miscellaneous arrangements) run by a variety of ranks of governors, governor generals, viceroys, and lord lieutenants. British Crown colonies might have locally elected representative councils (Ceylon, Jamaica), nominated councils (Hong Kong), or simply direct rule by the governor (Singapore). British India was run by a civil service based on the Chinese system, initially open only to British nationals. Different colonies were variously administered by three separate government ministries in London (the Colonial Office, the India Office, the Foreign Office), and almost every colony had its own *ad hoc* form of administration locally (North America alone in the seventeenth century had its Charter, Proprietary, and Royal colonies). Two other elements combined to cement control: garrisons of military forces which could be deployed in case of resistance, often consisting of local soldiers with British officers, and the institution of a common legal system which at the upper levels would be conducted in English and administered by British judges and magistrates.

Two Models of Empire

Fundamentally, there have been two models for the governance of empire, those of assimilation or association, based on the alternative possibilities of uniformity or difference. The Roman, the Russian, the Portuguese, the French, the American, and the Japanese nominally at least pursued uniformity and assimilation. Those empires administered according to a principle of diversity included the Mongol Empire under Genghis Khan, the Ottomans, the Mughals, the British, the Dutch, and the German. In practice, none of them kept strictly to this division, but the general difference between them holds true. Within these models, most nineteenth-century imperialists distinguished between the spheres of settlement and of rule, of colonization and domination, or, as British commentators liked to put it, between their Greek and their Roman colonies – in other words, what are now called settler and exploitation colonies (Osterhammel 1997; Veracini 2010).

Assimilation is best suited to land empires: in modern times Napoleon established the model on Enlightenment principles. This involved the attempt to impose a degree of cultural unity and uniformity throughout, with appropriated territories incorporated (paradoxically) within the nation-state, obliged to speak the imperial language and to operate under a common legal code. As the French themselves were to discover, the doctrine of assimilation was more difficult to enforce in the case of maritime empires, but the real problem was that over time their Republican fervor for the idea of equality throughout the empire declined in the face of increasing racism.

Inevitably, both systems can be seen to have their relative positives and negatives. On the one hand, uniformity, often accompanied by the incorporation of the overseas territory into the metropolitan state, as in the case of most land empires and the French, the Italian, or the Japanese maritime empires, is generally more politically equitable, extending (in theory, at least) the benefits of the nation to all the populations of the empire as if it were an expanded nation. The French colonies became simply *départements*, albeit *d'outre mer*, of France itself. Even today, Martinique and Guadeloupe in France are part of the territory of France (the Dutch Antilles, however, can claim to be the most westward territory of the European Union, the most eastward being France's Réunion in the Indian Ocean, the first country to use the Euro). This imperial policy of settlement and assimilation was one of the reasons why Algeria, technically a part of France, proved so hard to decolonize. The guiding theoretical assumption of the assimilation model is that all people are part of the same human species and share a common humanity, and that inequality between them can be eradicated by an education system run according to the principles and protocols of the imperial power. Any idea of a hierarchical system of racial difference is (in theory, at least) denied, though this was very seldom the case in practice.

On the other hand, the project of assimilation, or at worst the ethno-centric project of the *mission civilisatrice* pursued by France, inevitably involves the destruction of local cultures, languages, and religions, sometimes even the people themselves. The *mission civilisatrice* can easily be turned into an assumption of racial as well as cultural superiority, with little respect for other ethnicities, their customs and traditions, all regarded as inferior – in short, with no tolerance of cultural difference. Those who insist on maintaining their own culture, language, or religion often suffered discrimination, as in French Algeria or Portuguese Angola. The most extreme examples of this attitude would be the Spanish and Portuguese empires, which practiced forced religious conversion. In Algeria, the French carried out forced unveilings of women. In practice, as time went on, imperial powers such as France and Portugal became distinctly less enthusiastic about the doctrine of assimilation that was foundational to their ideology of the *mission civilisatrice*. Whereas in 1848 full civil and political rights, including voting rights, were given to former slaves in the Antilles, Réunion, and Guiana, as well as to natives from the French territories of India and from certain cities in Senegal, by the end of the century it was practically impossible for natives from Algeria or Indochina to obtain French citizenship, even if in legal terms they possessed all the qualifications that should have allowed them to do so (Saada 2012: 108–115). The historic discrimination within late French colonial practice between the people living in the same territory with the status of *indigène* and that of *citoyen français* has been recalled and highlighted since 2005 in the provocative, oxymoronic name of the radical French political organization Mouvement des Indigènes de la République (MIR). For their part, the assimilative ideology of *luso-tropicalismo* notwithstanding (Young 2006), the Portuguese themselves estimated the proportion of "natives" and *assimilados* in colonial Angola to be approximately 99 percent to 1 percent (Bragança and Wallerstein 1982: 1, 75).

The empires of Britain, Holland, and the Ottoman Empire, on the other hand, were constructed very differently, on principles that were the very reverse of assimilationist. In general in these empires, while there would be an imperial language for administration, which was often also used in at least one tier of the legal system, in other respects the diverse cultures of the empires were allowed to remain in place, or even encouraged to develop autonomously (in Malta, for example, the British encouraged the official use of the Maltese language, albeit in the desire to stop the use of Italian). The British rarely claimed they were bringing civilization: what they claimed to offer was the rule of law, the special attribute of their own society and its institutions, formulated definitively in the nineteenth century by the jurist A. V. Dicey (Bingham 2010). The claim for the establishment of the rule of law, along with human rights, remains unchanged and unchallenged in the West today, effectively combining the two imperial models (Brooks 2003; Ginsburg 2011). Along with the rule of law as the foundation of the colonial state, came the maintenance of order and the creation of infrastructures such as the building of railways and the provision of a postal service, all designed to ensure peace and stability and to facilitate trade and commerce. However, the principle of cultural respect, of non-interference in local cultures, in this model, which at one level seems much more liberal and enlightened, could also be predicated on an assumption of a fundamental difference between the civilized and the savage, of racial inferiority, of the inherent inadequacy of other peoples, who would never be in a position to be equal and who were therefore not even worth educating beyond the most basic level. It was easy in this situation to conflate race with class assumptions, for the British also assumed that their own lower classes, as well as those of the empire, were not up to being educated, or argued that giving them knowledge would be dangerous for political stability (which was probably, indeed, the case). As a result, the British preferred to run their colonies by indirect rule, using local authorities and allowing the continuation of local customs, without enforcing British culture upon them in the manner of the French, a technique of administering empire that goes back to the use of satraps by Cyrus the Great. In that respect, their practice was closer to that of the Dutch or the Ottomans. In practice, local cultures were not left completely untouched. Recent historians (Bayly 1996; Chatterjee n.d.) have argued that what the British administrators interpreted as Hindu or African customary law, for example, was often the result of their own expectations, as well as conforming to the agendas of local informants. In any case, such systems were usually combined with the British system of common law, using the English language, and enforcing basic British legal principles such as property rights, the prohibition of slavery, and, perhaps paradoxically, of tolerance.

Similar arguments about the ways in which imperial rule transformed the basis of local cultures can be made with respect to the creation of tribes and tribal identities, religion as a basis of political identity, and much more (Mamdani 2002).

Both models of empire drew on the historical example of the Roman Empire because all Europeans in the modern period assumed that the spread of Roman civilization had indeed brought civilization to the rest of Europe, that the infrastructure of roads and public buildings that the Romans created across Europe had been an undeniable public good, even if at the cost of the local cultures of the "barbarian" tribes. But who now cared about them? As Marlow comments in Joseph Conrad's *Heart of Darkness* during a conversation that takes place on a boat on the Thames in London, "And this also … has been one of the dark places of the earth" (Conrad 1902: 54). However, as C. P. Lucas observed in 1912 (Lucas 1912, I: 309), there was a fundamental difference between the Roman and the later European empires: the question of color and the organization of empire according to the principle of race. The discriminatory practices predicated on ideas of racial prejudice provided both the mechanism of imperial governance and administration and the ultimate reason for imperial downfall, since it was race that determined the difference between those colonies that were allowed independence and autonomy, and those that continued to be ruled autocratically, albeit on a principle of trusteeship. White settler colonies were allowed self-government, even when whites were in a minority, as in South Africa, whereas no non-white colony was ever allowed more than a representative council, under the overall rule of the governor. The ease with which settler colonies were given autonomy, indeed sometimes coerced unwillingly into autonomy, as in the case of the 1901 federation of Australia (Western Australia then tried to secede in 1933), that was denied everywhere else looks, in retrospect, extraordinary and contradictory.

Empires and Diversity

How did empires manage the diversity of their immense territories? Being so extensive in geographical terms, empires by definition have almost always included a vast variety of different peoples, with different

languages, religions, cultures, and customs. Confronting and administering multiplicity was fundamental to empire: from today's perspective, how empires dealt with heterogeneity can be seen as one of the
most interesting things about them. One response, as we have seen, was
to try to eradicate it through the policy of assimilation, in which the
empire became a part of the nation-state and shared its precepts – most
famously, perhaps, in the phrase that all schoolchildren were taught
to repeat in schools throughout the French Empire – "our ancestors,
the Gauls...."

In those empires that took the opposite course, difference was
actively promoted, beginning with a cultivated distinction between the
ruler and the ruled, which was easily facilitated if there was a significant
cultural or physical dissimilarity between them, which in turn was tied
to the assumption of a racial hierarchy. In this situation, diversity was
governed according to a theory of rank, which provided the measure
whereby different constituencies could be treated equitably and differently at the same time (Cannadine 2001). The British in India also took
over the Muslim system of law that had been established under the
Mughal emperors, with separate systems of customary or personal law
for those of different religions: diversity was managed by specific
arrangements for various constituencies at the local level, though as
has already been stated, the British hybridized this arrangement by
adding a further upper layer of British common law. In the same
way, in representative forums there were distinct constituencies for
different religions. Though the British are often criticized for their
divide-and-rule policies in India, or even blamed for the origin of
Hindu–Muslim sectarianism, the system that they applied was already in
place – indeed, the Muslim system of law continues there today. Other
empires tolerating religious diversity included the Russian, and in
earlier times, the Achaemenid Empire of Cyrus the Great, and the
Mongol Empire of Genghis Khan, famous for its strict code of law
practiced throughout the empire. The difference between imperial
intolerance and tolerance is most dramatically illustrated by the
contrast between the multi-faith culture of Córdoba when part of al-
Andalus under Muslim rule (Anidjar 2002), and its subsequent fate
under Ferdinand and Isabella after the Christian *Reconquista* of 1492,
when Jews and Muslims were expelled from Spain. The Spanish

Inquisition was created at that time to ensure the orthodoxy of those who had converted from Judaism and Islam. By contrast, when the Ottomans captured Constantinople in 1453, Sultan Mehmed II allowed the orthodox Christian church to continue to practice. Ottoman religious tolerance, so different from European religious intolerance in this period, was one of the factors that would encourage the later development of ideas of tolerance in Europe (Young 2012). In 2012, over five hundred years after the *Reconquista*, Spain finally apologized to the Jews (but not the Muslims) and offered those with Sephardic heritage Spanish citizenship.[5] In 2015, Portugal followed suit.

Whatever their mode of governance, and whether tolerant of cultural diversity or not, the majority of empires, including the Roman, were continually challenged from without or within. Most of the European empires existed in a state of almost perpetual war as resisting "rebels," "traitors," and "terrorists" around the world were "pacified," to use the imperial language. At the same time, whereas older empires had been for the most part dictatorial, and accepted as such, the European empires, also fundamentally authoritarian, were confronted by a developing liberal consensus among progressives at home and within the colonies that endorsed concepts of freedom and emancipation, of the nation and self-determination. From a longer-term perspective, the ideas that would be embodied in the American and French revolutions effectively made empires unsustainable; yet anachronistically the apex of imperialism, so mighty and yet so fragile, would develop almost a century later.

Notes

1   In the case of the British Empire, the term was first proposed by the Elizabethan scholar John Dee in the sixteenth century. After the accession of James VI of Scotland to the English throne in 1603, "British Empire" was used to describe the British Isles. By the eighteenth century, the term was used in its modern sense of British possessions and dependencies around the world (OED).

2   Osterhammel (1997: 17) calls them "maritime enclaves," but this leaves out land garrisons such as air bases.

3 http://www.theguardian.com/world/2014/jul/09/files-uk-role-cia-rendition-destroyed-diego-garcia-water-damage.
4 Many native American nations, of course, remained independent right through into the nineteenth century, though whether they could be described as states is another question.
5 http://www.bbc.co.uk/news/magazine-21631427.

3

Colony

The Temporality of Colonization

If there have broadly been three kinds of colonies – settlement, exploitation, and garrison – all colonies differ in turn with respect to the duration of their submission to colonial rule. The times and temporalities of colonization varied dramatically, from hundreds of years for Goa, Ireland, and Macau, to scarcely fifty in the case of Nigeria. Even so, Nigeria would not exist in its present form had it never been part of the British Empire. Periods of colonial rule were often highly unstable: some colonies were only ever controlled by one European state, but for others there were changes of rulers: before the nineteenth century, Caribbean colonies were frequently the object of international power struggles, seized by one country then appropriated by another; the Americas were variously colonized by the Portuguese, the Spanish, the French, the Dutch, the English, and, less well known, also by Couronians, Danes, Germans, Italians, the Knights of Malta, Norsemen, Russians, Swedes, and Scots; Sri Lanka was successively ruled by the Portuguese, the Dutch, and the British; while China was colonized (through "concessions" and extraterritorial zones) by almost every country that had any aspirations to international power at the beginning of the twentieth century. Colonies with changing rulers were not necessarily just outside Europe: in 1792 Poland was partitioned by Russia, Prussia, and Austria

Empire, Colony, Postcolony, First Edition. Robert J. C. Young.
© 2015 Robert J. C. Young. Published 2015 by John Wiley & Sons, Ltd.

and ceased to exist for over a hundred years. Independence was restored from 1918 until 1939, when Poland was invaded by Germany, Slovakia, and the Soviet Union; after World War II it was governed under the umbrella of the Soviet Union until 1989.

The word "colony" itself has changed over time. The underlying shift in all languages in the twentieth century was from a relatively positive to a negative connotation, reflecting the degree to which colonies are now regarded as negating the rights of local, indigenous, or aboriginal peoples, and empires seen as despotic systems in an age of democracy. Was the colony a particular European invention? The development of overseas colonies by Europeans from the fifteenth century onward can be linked back to the creation of Greek colonies detached from the Greek mainland in classical times. It was, however, the later colonies of European nations, intrinsically related to empire but also conceptually distinct, that established the modern notions both of a "colony" and, as a result, of "colonialism."

The Colony as Settlement

The Greek term for colony was originally *apoikia*, or settlement (literally "people far from home"). Greek *apoikiai* were city-states established all over the Mediterranean made up of emigrants who retained their cultural ties with the *metropolis* or home city. Each colony, however, was politically autonomous and functioned as an independent *polis*, or city-state. The Romans, for their part, used the Latin term *colonia* in two related ways: drawing on the meaning of *colonus* as farmer, it designated a settlement, or farm estate, often granted to veteran soldiers in conquered territories, initially in regions relatively close to Rome but intended to act as outposts to defend Roman territory. In time, these settlements also came to include towns that were assigned a comparably favored rank on the basis of their population of Roman citizens: Roman *coloniae* included Ostia (the first), London, Bath, York, Arles, Köln, Narbonne, and Jerusalem, cities established at the farthest reaches of the empire over various periods in order to act in some degree as imperial garrisons. For this reason, Roman authors also used the term *colonia* to translate the Greek *apoikia*. However, the specific function of the *coloniae* as strategic outposts of the Roman Empire meant that later Greeks did not translate the word back into their own language but rather employed the Latin *colonia* as a Greek term: *kolonia*. It was this Roman word with its particular political and strategic resonance that then entered French (fourteenth century) and English (sixteenth century) to designate settlements abroad. The term "plantation," to describe the planting of people as well as seeds, specifically in "a conquered or dominated country," was first used in English in 1587, and is recorded in 1610 with specific reference to Ulster (OED). The word "settlement," on the other hand, meaning to people or colonize a new country, was not employed until 1827. However, the verb "to settle," meaning to establish a colony, was already in operation a century earlier; one of its earliest recorded occurrences comes in an entry in the diary of John Evelyn in 1700, where he notes that the English "Parliament voted against the Scots invading or settling in the Darien" (OED). The colony, already under siege by the Spanish, was abandoned two months later. It was the financial failure of the Company of Scotland Trading to Africa and the Indies, which had drawn in a fifth of the available capital of Scotland to set up a Scottish colony called New Caledonia in Panama, still today called Puerto Escocés, that led to the Act of Union with England in 1707 and a bailout of the shareholders (Watt 2007). Evelyn's phrase here, "invading or settling," nicely brings out the contradiction with respect to colonial settlement that can never be eliminated: in order to settle, you have to invade.

The Greek practice of autonomous colonies did not survive the creation of the Roman Empire: colony and empire ever since have retained an unbroken identification of each with the other, even if that relation has often been one of tension and conflict. While colony comprises the individual settlement, empire includes the totality of settlements from the point of view of the metropolis which is the center of imperial administration. The majority of modern European colonies were formed on the Roman political model, involving the founding of a settlement in a separate, usually overseas, locality which sought to expand the territory and reduplicate or renew the culture of the parent country ("New" Amsterdam, England, Spain, York, etc.) while retaining allegiance to it and submitting to its overall political control. This was the basis of the settlers in British North America. The model of sovereignty in this period meant that, in contrast to ancient Greece, individuals remained subjects of the Crown (and therefore of the law of the state) wherever they might happen to be in the world (Benton 2010). The Pilgrim Fathers and their successors still thought of themselves as English, subjects of the Crown, however much they may have emigrated in order to practice freely their fundamentalist version of Protestantism.

Such settlement was originally the enterprise of groups of individuals, corporations, joint-stock companies, or other organizations, rather than initiated directly by states. The state was typically more interested in trade, through funding exploration expeditions aimed at locating places suitable for resource extraction or licensing trading companies to trade in luxury commodities. A different kind of colony consequently developed in the form of trading posts (the Greeks had distinguished between the *apoikiai* and their trading posts for which they used a different word, *emporiai*), which in many cases then gradually took on territorial scope. A prime example would be that of the East India Company, which expanded from its original trading outpost (which became the city of Calcutta) to control the whole of India. Such colonies, where trade, resource extraction, or port facilities were primary, rather than settlement, were those now referred to as "exploitation" colonies. While many early European colonies were "settler colonies," these were generally restricted to regions where Europeans could establish themselves more easily. Settlement only took place in colonies with temperate climates where Europeans could survive. It was widely believed that in tropical countries, even if Europeans were able to stay alive, it was impossible for them to procreate through several generations without returning to their homeland, or alternatively by mixing with native "stock." For this reason, with the exception of the Caribbean and South America, where racial mixing was widespread, Europeans rarely settled in intemperate climes. British people did not go to settle in India – there were always comparatively few of them in the subcontinent, and most returned sooner or later to where they had come from in the British Isles. In the Caribbean, where the primary form of settlement took the form of the creation of plantations, many plantation owners in fact never left Europe at all, or at most came to visit for short periods (for example, the dilettante novelist William Beckford, reputed at one point to be the richest man in England on the proceeds of his slave estates in Jamaica, or Sir Thomas Bertram, in Jane Austen's *Mansfield Park* (1814), who visits his estates in Antigua during the course of the novel). For the most part, however, in practice in the Caribbean the immigrant European and African populations, masters and slaves, together with the remaining indigenous natives, progressively became more mixed, "creolized." The same thing happened, in different degrees, in South America, most of all in Mexico and Brazil. In other South American states, such as Argentina, Bolivia, and Chile, the descendants of European settlers tried more diligently to cling on to the vestiges of their European cultural and racial identities.

Colonization, Migration, and Indigenous Peoples

Colonization, therefore, as practiced and conceptualized in Europe, was at once a trading enterprise, a quest for resources, and a form of migration of people who left their homelands and established themselves elsewhere in the prospect of a better life. However, unlike migration today, in conceptual and imaginative terms colonization included little sense of there being anyone else who already lived in the new land. Whereas in the twenty-first century migration involves the migrant going to a fully established host country in which he or she will participate, in earlier times colonization implied that a group from a particular society would displace themselves to an uninhabited space where they would develop and maintain their own culture, while generally retaining a distant political allegiance to the state from which they had come. The primary aim of most colonists was simply migration and settlement, not to rule other peoples. The Zionist idea of a land without people for people without land was the implicit motto of all early colonizers, authorized by John Locke's definitive philosophical and legal formulation whereby it was premised that land had to be settled for it to be considered occupied. In this characterization, designed in part to allow for the private appropriation of common land in England, nomadic people such as Native Americans were judged to have no inherent right to the land which they inhabited. Colonization was thus premised on what some have argued was the relatively new idea of individuals "owning" land (Linklater 2014).

While the idea of settlement and ownership was fundamental to the ideology of colonization, in most cases the land was in fact already occupied even if not in a way recognized by the colonizers, and so when they found themselves competing over territory colonizers in general simply moved the indigenous people out, usually by force or extermination, or sometimes inadvertently by bringing new diseases to which native inhabitants were inevitably particularly vulnerable (Bailyn 2013). Treaties with local inhabitants were also made, but usually only to be broken. Only in rare cases such as New Zealand's Treaty of Waitangi, signed in 1840 after the British Crown required the colonists to negotiate with the indigenous Maori, are there treaties to which contemporary indigenous peoples can appeal. However, even in New Zealand, the treaty was more or less ignored by the government until the 1970s – when it suddenly discovered that its country had been renamed by Maori activists Aotearoa/New Zealand.

The lack of legal title is a universal problem for the claims of indigenous people to their land that continues to this day: the colonists, themselves ruling by fiat and force rather than by right, brought their own particular written system with them which became the established law, while their courts characteristically favored the claims of the settlers, as in Israel/Palestine today (Shehadeh 1985). The native inhabitants often lacked the "proper" legal proof that they owned the land which they had inherited – a proof almost impossible to provide since their rights were being determined according to a completely different exotic legal system that was alien to their culture (Belmessous 2014). The appropriation of land and the counter-claim to what in Australia is now called "native title" has been and continues to be one of the key issues in colonial and postcolonial states. One notable feature was that annexation of land often became more marked after independence than before – as in the United States, or in South Africa where the notorious 1913 Natives' Land Act, which effectively debarred Africans from owning land, even if they already owned it, was enacted just three years after the creation of the Union of South Africa. Although there has been some restitution since 1993, unresolved aspects of the history of land appropriation remain fundamental to South African politics today.

Colonizers for the most part did not choose to settle because of any imperial ideology, though they mostly lived according to one once they

[handwritten margin note: forced laws & language on Indians]

arrived. A large number of the millions who left Europe to colonize other parts of the world did so for the same reason most people migrate today: economic need. They were themselves often victims – of persecution or poverty, or of being forced to migrate by their landlords, or because they had broken the law, often as a result of their poverty or beliefs. Historically, this situation does not seem to have made migrants more compassionate with respect to indigenous populations that they then encountered elsewhere – in fact, the historical record often indicates the opposite. Indigenous colonized people always seem prone to become the victims of the victims.

The geographical violence of land appropriation was often accompanied by physical violence toward native inhabitants: by killing them (such as the massacre of the Charrúa people in Uruguay in the 1830s), or evicting them (such as the forced removal of the Cherokees in 1838 along the Trail of Tears to Indian Territory, modern Oklahoma), or by using them as labor, since once the colonists had appropriated the land, they needed people to work it. This was realized through forms of compulsory work schemes that employed contemporary practices in Europe and many other places around the world: serfdom and slavery. In later centuries after the abolition of slavery, forced labor was achieved through less direct methods, taking forms such as indentured or bonded labor or, in Africa, hut taxes designed to compel the hut dwellers to sell their labor in order to pay the tax. The use of unfree labor, at worst sustained through forced migration and the deprivation of all social, cultural, and political rights as in the case of slavery, inevitably produced a society in which differences between colonizer and laborer were then reified in cultural terms constructed to match the political conditions of power. The basis of this difference was anchored not in the institution of class, as it had been in Europe, but in the concept of race.

Colonizer and Colonized: Intimate Enemies

Colonial rule inevitably created the distinction between colonizer and colonized, between colonials and colonial subjects. This division masks the fact that in settlement colonies there were really three groups: the colonized natives, the colonial rulers who came from the metropolitan center, and the settlers (*colons*). The difference between the last two rested on class and identity: the colonial rulers would originate from and return to the metropole, while the settlers, many of whom may not have even been the same nationality as the colonial rulers, were settled, and identified with the colony as their home. They had usually come there as a result of poverty or forced migration, and though colonials, were in some degree both colonizers and colonized. As colonizers they might oppress the indigenous population, force them to labor on their behalf, drive them off their lands, or simply slaughter them. In some colonies in the Caribbean, they might also develop cultural similarities with them – "creolization" – so that in some ways they might identify more with them than with their own leaders. As colonials living permanently in the colony, they might in turn feel oppressed by the colonial rulers and metropolitan government, who were not helping them enough, taxing them too much, providing inadequate defense from the natives, or, worse, insisting on their fair and decent treatment. In terms of class and culture, settler colonials knew that they were seen as inferior by those back "home," even while they looked to the metropole as the basis of their own identity. From the point of view of the indigenous colonized natives, on the other hand, there was little distinction between the two groups of colonials – rulers and settlers – since they were fundamentally on the same side. From their perspective, independence for the colony simply put the settlers in power as a racial elite, as in Australia, Aotearoa/New Zealand, Chile, Peru, or South Africa. In such settler colonies, colonial rule was followed by sovereignty which for indigenous people simply initiated another form of colonial rule in perpetuity. The status of indigenous peoples in current or former colonies remains one of the most obvious "postcolonial" political issues. What exactly, though, makes a people "indigenous?" We shall return to this question in chapter 11.

Once local resistance had been "pacified," and the colony established, native and settler, or native and colonial ruler, were required in some degree to live together, experiencing each other, in Ashis Nandy's memorable phrase, as "the intimate enemy" (Nandy 1983). Colonizer and colonized were locked into a close relationship in which each was observing and trying to outwit the other (Memmi 1967). The division between them insisted on by the colonizer required some special physical arrangements, a different and distinctive spatial order to maintain the distance between them. The Martiniquan psychologist and anticolonial activist Frantz Fanon offers the most memorable description of the urban geography of colonialism, which rests on a fundamental structure of segregation:

> The colonial world is a world cut in two. The dividing line, the frontiers are shown by barracks and police stations. In the colonies, it is the policeman and the soldier who are the official, instituted go-betweens, the spokesmen of the settler and his rule of oppression …
>
> The zone where the native lives is not complementary to the zone inhabited by the settlers. … The settler's town is a strongly built town, all made of stone and steel. It is a brightly lit town; the streets are covered with asphalt, and the garbage cans swallow all the leavings, unseen, unknown and hardly thought about. … The town belonging to the colonized people, or at least the native town, the Negro village, the medina, the reservation, is a place of ill fame, peopled by men of evil repute. They are born there, it matters little where or how; they die there, it matters not where, nor how. It is a world without spaciousness; men live there on top of each other, and their huts are built one on top of the other. (Fanon 1966: 31–32)

Fanon was thinking of colonial Algeria in this evocative description of the compartmentalized urban landscape that was developed under the rule of the *colons*. Today, such a juxtaposition of two divided zones is most visible in the Occupied Territories in the West Bank in Palestine, where the Jewish settlements are built onto the landscape with high concrete walls dividing them from the overcrowded towns and villages of the Palestinians, accessed by special sealed-off highways to which local Palestinians have no access. While the question of whether Israel itself constitutes a settler colony has been fiercely debated, it is hard to argue that the Occupied Territories, by the very name that is most widely used for them, along with the language of "settlers" and "settlements," do not constitute a late-modern settler colony in a formal and political sense (Aaronsohn 1996; Mbembe 2003: 27–30, 39; Rodinson 1973; Veracini 2006).

The Colony as Trading Factory

Colonial rule brought different kinds of transformation: the most extreme forms of destruction and transformation of the landscape came in those parts of the Americas and the Caribbean where the indigenous population was almost exterminated and the land transformed into plantations worked by slaves and indentured or "bound" servants, transported from Africa, Ireland, and elsewhere (O'Callaghan 2001). The terms often used for this process, invented by the French philosopher Gilles Deleuze and psychiatrist Félix Guattari, are "deterritorialization" and "reterritorialization" (Deleuze and Guattari 1988: 432–435). These words emphasize the fact that the force of empire was deployed as much on the ecology as on the people who inhabited it (Crosby 2003, 2004). The more the physical landscape was altered, and the more the local economy was transformed, then the more penetrating was the cultural influence and transmutation. The Cuban anthropologist Fernando Ortiz in his 1941 book *Cuban Counterpoint* described this as a process of "transculturation." He wrote:

> I have chosen the word *transculturation* to express the highly varied phenomena that have come about in Cuba as a result of the extremely complex transmutations of culture that have taken place here, and without a knowledge of which it is impossible to understand the evolution of the Cuban folk, either in the economic or in the institutional, legal, ethical, religious, artistic, linguistic, psychological, sexual, or other aspects of its life.
>
> The real history of Cuba is the history of its intermeshed transculturations. (Ortiz 1995: 98)

Even in exploitation colonies, though change was less dramatic, colonial administrations forced revolutions in the areas of law, language, and education, or in other areas, such as the standardization of time, at the same time imposing cultural values in which culture itself was regarded as something European.

As Ortiz demonstrates, transformation did not only take place in the colonies, however. Colonies were the mechanisms for the global export of populations and circulation of goods. The effect was to transform the economies of Europe almost as much as that of the colony: not only abundant gold and silver, but also china, potatoes, sugar, tea, tobacco, and tomatoes changed European cultures forever. In more than just a political sense, for Europe, colonies became inadvertent agents of revolution. As Marx and Engels put it in *The Communist Manifesto* (1848):

> The discovery of America, the rounding of the Cape, opened up fresh ground for the rising bourgeoisie. The East Indian and Chinese markets, the colonization of America, trade with the colonies, the increase in the means of exchange and in commodities generally, gave to commerce, to navigation, to industry, an impulse never before known, and thereby, to the revolutionary element in the tottering feudal society, a rapid development. The feudal system of industry, in which industrial production was monopolized by closed guilds, now no longer sufficed for the growing wants of the new markets. The manufacturing system took its place. (Marx and Engels 2002: 220)

Marx and Engels here emphasize the dramatic effect on European society of the development of European global imperialism as a form of economic development that initiated industrialization. From the first, the colonies themselves were exporters of commodities, all of which in different ways transformed the economies and culture of Europe, gold and silver in particular initially helping to ease a lack of liquidity that was the result of a trade deficit with the East, and to provide capital for industrialization, albeit at the cost of inflation. However, the economics of circulation took some time to match up: while populations (and slaves) flowed westwards, capital tended to flow eastwards: silver carried from South America to Europe was used to pay for Chinese tea and porcelain, creating a trade deficit that eventually led to the Opium Wars of 1839–42 and 1856–60. It was around this time that imperialists in the metropole began to put the export of people and goods together. It seemed like a virtuous circle: unwanted populations at home could be exported as settlers to become a market for European industrial products, while they in turn would send their raw commodities to Europe. For much of the colonial period (whether under mercantilism or the later nineteenth-century imperial preference systems), access to colonial markets was therefore strictly controlled, always organized in favor of the imperial power. For a period after the abolition of the Corn Laws in 1846, the British championed free trade, with liberals claiming that it also promoted peace. In the twenty-first century, under a rather different global arrangement, and under the moniker of neoliberalism, the drive for free trade remains in place.[1]

The Colony as the Laboratory of Modernity

Transformed by force, the colony could also become a laboratory of experiment for new technology and new ways of thinking. In the early 1800s the British East India Company became dominated by radical utilitarians who put their thinking to work in India in experimental form long before utilitarianism affected the political organization of Britain itself (Stokes 1959). The enduring assumption, however, was that it was Europe that was most "developed" and the colonies that were some sort of rural retreat – a retreat to which aesthetes who deplored industrialization could escape. The remote backwater certainly describes some colonies, as V. S. Naipaul testifies in his account of Mr Biswas' life in Trinidad – though the novel ends with the discovery of oil (Naipaul 1961). This was not, however, always the case: when European colonization began, China and India were the primary manufacturing countries in the world; even in 1800 half of the world's manufacturing still took place there (Allen 2011: 7). All that was transformed by the European industrial revolution, itself in part enabled by the influx of capital from South America and the transfer of high-heat technology from China (Goody 2012). Once colonized, industrialization as such was generally discouraged as competition to industrial Europe, and established manufacturing industries in the colony were often destroyed as a result of the importation of cheap European manufactured goods, such as English printed cloth in India. In some areas, however, such as agriculture in Algeria, or engineering in the Dutch East Indies, industrialization in the colonies was far in advance of the still traditional practices in Europe (Mrazek 2002). Moreover, as C. L. R. James pointed out in 1938, the tobacco or sugar plantation run on slave labor was in one sense the first factory, operating as a first-run for the capitalist instrumental organization of human labor, the first example of the factory system of the industrial revolution ("Fordism") in which humans were made completely subservient to the machine:

> When three centuries ago the slaves came to the West Indies, they entered directly into the large-scale agriculture of the sugar plantation, which was a modern system. It … required that the slaves live together in a social relation far closer than any proletariat of the time.… The cane when reaped had to be rapidly transported to what was factory production. The product was shipped abroad for sale. Even the cloth the slaves wore and the food they ate was imported. The Negroes, therefore, from the very start lived a life that was in its essence a modern life. (James 2001: 305–306)

As James argues, forms of modernity were sometimes developed in the colonies in advance of the metropole. Attempts to differentiate colonial modernity into modernities, however, miss the point that modernity itself was produced by the expansion of Europe around the world and the reciprocal effects of that globalization on Europe itself. In other words, it was not that modernity was produced in Europe and then exported, rather that modernity was itself produced by the export of Europe and import of colonial wealth with reciprocal effects around the world, in Europe as elsewhere. The emergence of modernity was intimately connected with the colonial project (Hardt and Negri 2000).

One of the other forms of that modernity was militarization, as a result of the almost constant wars fought by colonial powers to repress colonial insurrections. These were often useful in developing new technologies and techniques of war, particularly air power – the newly formed RAF's first bombing raid was conducted against Iraqis rebelling against their new colonial masters in 1920 (Omissi 1990; Hippler 2013). At the same time, a central feature of modernity was frequent war between the colonial powers themselves: from the first, the influx of money and goods from the newly established colonies, and the relative superficiality and instability of colonization, meant there was constant competition through war and piracy to appropriate the spoils of other European powers. From the sixteenth to the twentieth centuries, wars in Europe were frequently precipitated by colonial rivalries. The eighteenth century, for example, was dominated by wars fought out in colonial arenas, the objectives of which were the appropriation of each other's colonial territories. European wars, often extended globally, were colonial wars: their effect was the continuing transformation of the political landscape of Europe itself.

If colonization transformed its subject territories, therefore, at the same time the colonies transformed Europe. Along with almost constant war, colonization brought about radical economic, cultural, and physical changes. Wealth from the colonies, whether as silver or commodities, boosted the development of capitalism, which in turn shifted European class and economic structures and therefore its configurations of power. That new economic and political climate also generated the basis for a liberal society in which ideas of the Enlightenment would be developed, such as democracy, freedom, equality, and the nation-state, concepts that would in turn eventually make colonialism unsustainable. For this reason, some historians continue to argue that in its more benign forms in its later stages, colonialism could be seen as a positive force, bringing technology, education, healthcare, and the rule of law (Ferguson 2002). All of these arguments were already made eighty years before in Lord Lugard's *The Dual Mandate in British Tropical Africa* (1922). In that work, Lugard, echoing the passage from Conrad's *Heart of Darkness* cited in the previous chapter, put forward what became the classic defense of colonialism and the value of colonial rule, which he justified by what he called the "dual mandate" of mutual benefit:

As Roman imperialism laid the foundations of modern civilization, and led the wild barbarians of these islands [Britain] along the path of progress, so in Africa today we are repaying the debt, and bringing to the dark places of the earth, the abode of barbarism and cruelty, the torch of culture and progress, while ministering to the material needs of our own civilization. In this task the nations of Europe have pledged themselves to cooperation by a solemn covenant. Towards the common goal each will advance by the methods most consonant with its national genius. British methods have not perhaps in all cases produced ideal results, but I am profoundly convinced that there can be no question but that British rule has promoted the happiness and welfare of the primitive races. Let those who question it examine the results impartially. If there is unrest, and a desire for independence, as in India and Egypt, it is because we have taught the value of liberty and freedom, which for centuries these peoples had not known. Their very discontent is a measure of their progress. (Lugard 1922: 618)

In Lugard's account, even anticolonial agitation is appropriated and offered as one of the achievements of British imperialism. So too today, it is argued the British Empire was the only empire ever pledged to the principle of liberty (Greene 2009). Others have seen empire as an archaizing or tradition-inventing power that helped to create social cohesion and the stability of institutions (Hobsbawm and Ranger 1983). Marx, as we have seen, by contrast saw empire as inherently revolutionary and therefore to that extent, progressive in the long run.

Outside Europe, however, it is hard to persuade anyone that colonized people really benefited in any significant way from colonial rule. What Lugard and modern historians all pass over is the fundamental inequity of living in an empire whose organization and justification were founded on an ideology of race and racial superiority.

Note

1   Predictably, in a globalized world, a country's openness to free trade is now measured on an index: the Enabling Trade Index.

4

Slavery and Race

Slavery

Slavery was central to European colonialism from the earliest overseas empires of Spain and Portugal. There was nothing new about slavery: slavery has existed almost everywhere on earth at different times in many different forms and continues today, despite all legislation against it. Even its legal abolition is recent in some places – in Saudi Arabia, for example, slavery was only abolished in 1962, in Mauritania, 1981. By the time of the European empires, slavery was diminishing in Europe, while its close analogue, serfdom, was in the process of giving way to a freer peasantry, except in Russia. However, a custom that had been long-standing in Europe and the rest of the world, whereby those taken in war could be made slaves, still persisted, particularly if they were not of the same religion as the captor. Europeans themselves, including Miguel de Cervantes, author of *Don Quixote*, were taken as slaves from around the Mediterranean coast by Barbary pirates until the nineteenth century. By the sixteenth century slavery was not practiced widely within Europe, but it was still deemed acceptable to enslave non-Europeans who were non-Christians, particularly if they were kept outside Europe. The establishment of plantations, in Ireland and then in the Americas, reconfigured this practice dramatically. The annihilation of the indigenous peoples of the Americas through violence or disease,

Empire, Colony, Postcolony, First Edition. Robert J. C. Young.
© 2015 Robert J. C. Young. Published 2015 by John Wiley & Sons, Ltd.

or the refusal of those who survived to work for the conquistadors, produced a shortage of labor, with the result that from the beginning of the sixteenth century, African slaves started to be brought to the Caribbean and the Americas to work in the plantations. The first slave was brought by the Spanish to Hispaniola (now Haiti and the Dominican Republic) in 1501. Though slavery was technically outlawed in Spain and Portugal in the sixteenth century, it continued in Spanish Caribbean islands such as Cuba, where it was abolished only in 1886, or formerly Spanish colonies such as Chile (1811) or Venezuela (1845), or in formerly Portuguese Brazil (1888). Sweden gave freedom to its slaves in its Caribbean colony, Saint Barthélemy, in 1847. Slavery was not proscribed in the United States until the end of the Civil War in 1865, four years after the serfs were emancipated in Russia. One of the remarkable aspects of the history of slavery is that while it has been officially brought to an end at specific times in different places, in practice it has had to be stopped again and again, right up to the twenty-first century. Human trafficking of "disposable people" continually takes new forms, whether it be for sex work or the production of prawns, and has, so far, proved impossible to eradicate (Bales 2012). In 1807, in the *Phenomenology of Mind*, Hegel posed the radical question about slavery and its relation to freedom in the context of western history and political ideology: should we conceive of freedom as the final liberation of humankind, to which we are all progressing, or does freedom paradoxically require slavery in an irresolvable, unfinishable dialectical fashion (Buck-Morss 2009)?

Slavery was the most transformative of European colonial practices. If European colonies were different from those that had preceded them in the history of the world's empires by the very fact of their geographical dispersal, the same fact transformed the role of slavery within them. Whether transported by conquering armies, or across slave-trade routes, slavery constituted part of long-standing practices in Africa, the Ottoman Empire, India, East Asia, and the Americas before the arrival of Europeans. What was different about colonial slavery was that it did not form part of a local practice, but involved an industrial system of human trafficking in which millions of slaves were transported across the Atlantic Ocean in specially made ships to work in mines and plantations in the Americas. Although the various colonial powers regulated slavery in different ways (compare, for example, the loose regulations in the US slave states with the French *code noir*), the millions transported from the sixteenth to the nineteenth centuries were treated according to one ideological system, in which Africans, or to a lesser extent South and East Asians (including Chinese and Japanese), were not deemed fully human and therefore could be organized and treated according to a different moral and political system. However, true to the contradictory nature of the colony, it was in the places of slavery that some of the strongest advocates of liberty and human rights would emerge, applying such concepts to themselves and their own families, but not to their slaves. This moral contradiction formed the basis of the first major transnational political pressure group, the anti-slavery movement, which succeeded in effecting the abolition of the slave trade within the British Empire in 1807, followed by the abolition of slavery in 1833 (in practice, however, this was largely applied only to British Atlantic colonies). European colonization thus both instituted and then abolished the practice of transatlantic slavery, with slavery persisting longer in those countries that had achieved independence than those that remained colonies. One of the main reasons behind the Great Trek in South Africa of 1836–8, when the Boers left the Cape Colony to avoid British rule, was the British abolition of slavery and proclamation of equal legal rights for people of color. After 1807, the British worked actively to prevent the slave trade by policing the world's oceans and pressurizing other nations to put an end to slavery. Having made slavery illegal in India in 1841, British rulers there nevertheless then promoted indentured labor schemes around the world for Indians and Chinese whose conditions were often scarcely better (Huzzey 2012; Sherwood 2007).

A key moment in the history of slavery came in 1794 with the abolition of slavery within the French dominions, as an extension of the principles of the French Revolution. Notwithstanding Napoleon's subsequent attempts to reinstate it, the colony of Haiti led the first and only successful anticolonial slave revolt, achieving independence in 1804. Although no other slave colony was able to emulate Haiti's success, it nevertheless provided a persistent reminder of the contradictions between slavery and the Enlightenment political values that permeated the Americas (Buck-Morss 2009). Slavery was contested by constant slave revolts domestically, and by the anti-slavery movement transnationally. The anti-slavery movement represented the first international political campaign that succeeded in transforming law and policy throughout the world according to a humanitarian agenda. It served as the prototype for many later transnational political movements, such as the anti-Apartheid movement or contemporary indigenous, anti-globalization and ecological movements. In the nineteenth century, the arguments for the equal status of human beings made against slavery were extended to other issues such as gender equality, justice and civil liberty in the context of colonialism. How could liberty at home and autocracy abroad be justified other than according to the same kind of racialized thinking that had sustained the practice of slavery? Why should colonized people not have the same kind of human rights as the people in the countries that ruled them that professed to be founded on the principle of liberty? The abolition of slavery was, in many ways, the precursor to the abolition of colonialism itself.

Colonial rule therefore instituted the most traumatic form of slavery in human history, while colonial powers were also instrumental in initiating the international process to repress it. What remained was the cultural memory of slavery, particularly for the displaced African Americans in North and South America who had endured the dehumanizing process of being torn from their environments, families, culture, and language by the millions, many of whose descendants continue to live lives of deprivation and be subjected to social prejudice. At the same time, more positively, the culture of African Americans has been the most creative and influential of all those of the Americas, defining many of the forms and characteristics of North American culture as such. The callous circuits of the "Black Atlantic" would turn out to be the making of America in unexpectedly productive ways (Gilroy 1993).

Race

The anti-slavery movement, the defeat of the Confederates by the North in the United States, and the abolition of the slave trade and then of slavery itself, all signaled a shift away from extreme racism in which other races were designated as being outside the boundaries of humanity.

The idea of a common humanity ("am I not a man and a brother?") formed an inherently anti-racist agenda, even if it would not destroy the idea of racial hierarchy for many decades. While slavery was defeated on religious and humanitarian grounds during this period, it did not mean that Africans were henceforth treated as equals, or that the idea of race itself was discredited.

The ideology of race, which formalized racial prejudice into a system of thought and cultural value, was a colonial invention designed to justify slavery and authorize colonial rule. Although Hannah Arendt characterized only the Nazis with the term "race imperialism" (Young-Bruehl 2004), the phrase could justly be applied to all European and Japanese empires, for race provided the underlying ideological basis for imperial domination: in this way, modern empires differed from all those that had gone before them. Any attempt to compare positive and negative effects of modern colonialism must always begin by acknowledging that the system operated on a principle of racial prejudice. Modern colonialism was racist to the core, subjecting colonized peoples to the daily humiliation not just of subjugation, but of being treated as inferior beings.

Before Hitler, those who invented the discourse of race were not so up-front or even self-conscious about the aims of their project. In the context of slavery, however, they were: in the United States, Southern anthropologists writing before the Civil War such as Samuel George Morton, Josiah Nott, and George Gliddon, sought to defend the South's "peculiar institution" by developing an extensive racial ideology of the inferiority of non-white races, drawing on anthropological and anatomical arguments about race and culture from American and European doctors, anatomists, anthropologists, linguists, and historians. American racialists were most concerned with defining a hierarchy of races and racial abilities: they sought to prove the basis of racial distinction by comparing skull sizes, as well as claiming the inability of Africans ever to create a civilization, arguing that just as in nineteenth-century America, Africans had been slaves in every society since ancient Egypt (Young 1995).

The scientific study of race and racial difference, which began in Europe toward the end of the eighteenth century, offered a new way for Europeans to justify both slavery and European rule of non-Europeans.

This discourse of race emerged fully in the mid-nineteenth century, a little before the onset of the period of high imperialism. In earlier times, the term "race" had been used in a different context: a race was identified with the genealogical line of an individual aristocratic family. So an aristocrat without heirs would call himself the last of his race – as Horace Walpole's hero Manfred fears that he will be in *The Castle of Otranto* (1764). At that time, as the very fact of slavery suggests, what we would now call racism or racial prejudice certainly existed toward darker people ("moors," "gypsies") or Jews, but the focus for the grounds of their difference was placed not just on their physical differences but on their not being Christian. Neither was, or is, racism exclusively western, even institutionalized racism: the existence of caste systems in India, Ceylon (Sri Lanka), Japan, Korea, and Nepal, ensuring social stratification enforced by strict restrictions, very much suggests otherwise.

In the course of the eighteenth century, as trading and colonizing Europeans encountered many different peoples around the world, anatomists began to devote more and more attention to the topic of "comparative anatomy," that is, analysis of the physical anatomical difference between different peoples. While some anthropologists studied human diversity from the point of view of the variety of languages spoken, anatomists developed a classification system of the races of the world according to the characteristics of their bodies. In such accounts, they did not stop at describing physical difference, but associated anatomical classification with characteristics of moral and cultural difference in the manner of the tradition of books of comparative cultural anthropology that goes back as far as John Bulwer's *Anthropometamorphosis* (1650), reissued in 1654 as *A View of the People of the Whole World*. The European idea of culture inevitably provided the norm. As a result, races were not only classified on the basis of physical traits, but also put in a hierarchy in relation to cultural attainment, arranged according to their deviance from European civilization. So, broadly, the European was at the top of the hierarchy, Arabs, Indians, and Chinese somewhere lower down, Africans lower down still, and Australian aboriginals at the bottom. The knowledge that was invoked about these people was based on hearsay, reports from missionaries, sailors, and travelers, and not subject to anything like modern standard verification procedures. Derived from a relatively random and unsubstantiated set of evidence about the different peoples of the world whose authority grew as it was repeated from book to book, each racial theorist tried to make his (all racial theorists were male) mark by producing a different system of classification, for example in the overall number of races. The major topic of dispute was between the idea that all humans were one species (monogenesis), which correlated with the biblical account, and what was regarded as the progressive, scientific position that the different human races were in fact different species (polygenesis). The proof for the latter view was the claim that the progeny of interracial unions were infertile, which was linked to the idea of degeneration. So prevalent was the extremist view that races were inherently different species and that the current hierarchy would never change, that the only liberal response in the nineteenth century was to argue that education would allow other races to rise to the level of the European, as in the work of E. B. Tylor. The developmental schema was, in more than one sense, progressive. It was only at the beginning of the twentieth century that some anthropologists, notably Franz Boas, began to challenge the idea of race altogether (according to modern genetic science, the idea of race has no relation to the diverse DNA of different peoples).

The science of race as it was developed in the later nineteenth and twentieth centuries involved simple racial prejudice justified by what was accepted at that time as science. Such writings formed a closely knit branch of academic study, and were probably not read by many. But Europeans nevertheless came to know of them, so that the belief that ideas about racial difference were substantiated by scientific knowledge became widespread by the mid-nineteenth century. This occurred at the same time that European powers were increasingly colonizing and ruling lands occupied by "inferior" races, European colonial administrators were dealing directly with such people, and European governments legislating about the governance of their lives according to ideas which interweaved race with sexuality (Stoler 1995; Young 1995). Ideas of racial hierarchy, and the assumption that Europeans were superior to all other humans, fed conveniently into the European practice of appropriating the territory of others around the world, and subjecting the indigenous populations to various forms of treatment from extermination to political submission.

European scientists were equally interested in defining European "races" as a way of clarifying the true constituents of their own nations. In practice, even anthropologists found that European "races," as classified physically or documented by historical record, were very mixed. The French resolved the question by arguing that they were made up of two races, the Franks and the Gauls (the Franks, the aristocrats, were German by origin, while the Gauls were the indigenous Celtic peasants), which collated nicely with the idea of class hierarchy. The English, after an early attempt by historians at the time of the Napoleonic wars and the union with Ireland (1800) to argue that the true English were solely Protestant Saxons (or Teutons, i.e., Germans), were eventually reconciled to the idea that they were a mix of Saxons and Celts, with the hybrid mixture producing the distinctive qualities of the English and their culture (the term "British" was comparatively little used until the later twentieth century, but politically served a similar purpose) (Young 2008). Race was a particularly useful category for the Germans, who always had a problem in defining their nation by territory (no natural borders) or religion (Catholic and Protestant), or even language (hugely diverse in its various forms across Europe). Racial theory allowed the claim that all Germans belonged to the same Teutonic, later Aryan, race. One factor that complicated this national racial self-identification was the existence of a very substantial Jewish population in Europe, many of whom were also German or spoke a Yiddish that contained a strong Germanic element, particularly in its vocabulary and morphology: in response to Russian pogroms, and the relatively liberal policies of the Hapsburg Empire toward Jews in the nineteenth century, large numbers immigrated into Western Europe during this period. After the defeat of Germany in World War I, punished by reparations for alleged war guilt and the removal of its colonies, Adolf Hitler and the Nazi party blamed the presence of Jews in particular for Germany's ills. Employing a version of the racial theories that had been developed by anthropologists in the nineteenth century, Germany applied the principles of colonial rule to Europeans and became the first fully racialized state in Europe (Burleigh and Wippermann 1991). With industrial efficiency, Jews, gypsies, homosexuals, and other "deviants" were first expelled and then exterminated under the plan of the

"Final Solution," either in the death camps or by direct assassination by the Einsatzgruppen. After the invasion of Russia other races such as Slavs were starved to death, although the "Hunger Plan" for engineered famine was never coordinated or put into practice systematically. Similar policies based on a claimed racial typology were employed by the Japanese toward non-Japanese during the years of Japanese colonial expansion and invasion of Southeast Asia. After the defeat of Germany in 1945, and the discovery of the Nazi death camps, the idea of race was discredited by the international community through the United Nations and UNESCO (UNESCO 1969). What had been hitherto regarded as racial difference was reformulated as ethnicity, a loose word that gives more weight to cultural identity, though it may include factors such as physical similarity. Nations were encouraged to define themselves by other common factors, such as language and culture. With the exception of South Africa, which put a racialized system of apartheid into place after World War II, the assumption of a hierarchy of races was gradually challenged at the legal and cultural levels.

While Euro-American theories of race provided justification for empire, therefore, it was not until such theories of race were developed into extreme forms and consequences by the Nazis and applied to Europeans themselves that the whole edifice would be discredited. Authors such as Simone Weil and Hannah Arendt suggested that fascism was in fact nothing more than the methods of colonialism brought home and deployed on Europe itself.[1] Unlike Weil, however, Arendt did not intend to link race ideology to any other form of colonialism or imperialism, and by the time she published *Origins of Totalitarianism* in 1951 she would downplay the connection even between fascism and race imperialism in order to accommodate the Soviet Union in her critique of totalitarianism (Arendt 1958; Moses 2011; Tsao 2002; Young-Bruehl 2004: 203). Aimé Césaire, however, had already put the point bluntly in his *Discourse on Colonialism* (1950): "'Europe' is morally, spiritually indefensible … Hitler … applied to Europe colonialist procedures which until then had been reserved exclusively for the Arabs of Algeria, the coolies of India, and the blacks of Africa" (Césaire 1950: 8, 15–16; 1972: 1, 14). The ideology of colonialism and imperialism was broken.

Note

1 "Hitlerism consists in the application by Germany to the European continent, and more generally to the countries belonging to the white race, colonial methods of conquest and domination. The Czechs were the first to note this analogy when, protesting about the protectorate of Bohemia, they said 'No European people has ever been subjected to such a regime'" (Weil 2003: 110). Weil's essay, "The Colonial Question and the Destiny of the French People," was written in 1943, but not published until 1960.

5

Colonialism and Imperialism

We have seen that from the earliest days colonies, settlements, or trading posts abroad were established for a number of reasons: freedom of religion, need for land for surplus population, or desire to accumulate wealth through trade or the establishment of plantations. They tended to be created, as a result, on a relatively haphazard, pragmatic basis, driven by the needs of individuals, small groups, or licensed trading companies. Though they became components of particular empires, colonies were not generally planned from the outset as part of an imperial project, and there was often a degree of power struggle between a local desire for autonomy and control by the Crown to which they retained their nominal allegiance, as in the case of Britain's or Spain's American colonies.

Later colonies, especially in the nineteenth century, tended to be established as part of an imperial design. Empire involves universal rule by a sovereign power from the imperial center. Unless the empire is organized through indirect rule as separate fiefdoms, in some degree this requires a bureaucracy of sorts, loyal to the emperor, that will drive its priorities and require its laws to be obeyed throughout the empire. The rationale of empire is regional or global power, internal and external, and, as part of this, the accumulation of wealth. Nineteenth- or twentieth-century European empires did not essentially differ from this model. The word that came to be given to the imperial project as an idea driven from the metropolitan center at the highest level of the state itself was "imperialism." Imperialism was an overarching concept or ideology that openly advocated and practiced domination over the territories of other peoples of a different race. While colonization was the practice of actual settlement or occupation, the term "colonialism" is used to describe the colonial system that was put into operation in the colony itself, whereby non-Europeans, considered "backward" on racial grounds, were ruled and exploited by European (or Russian or Japanese) rulers or settlers. Colonies were the separate parts of empire, empire was the totality, the complete picture, seen as the product and possession of the imperial state and from its centered perspective. By the late nineteenth century, imperialism also came to be used to describe the development or maintenance of power ("hegemony") of one country over another through economic, diplomatic, and cultural domination even in the absence of direct colonial occupation.

Colonialism

When it was first introduced into English in the nineteenth century, the word "colonialism" retained the positive aura of the Roman *coloniae*. By 1919 it had come to be used as a derogatory term by its opponents, carrying the implication that all colonialism represented a form of exploitation of oppressed peoples by too powerful nations. In the twentieth century, colonialism became a negative word in the discourse of the widespread opposition to colonial rule by the native or indigenous people of the colonies. The older, more positive sense of colonial survives today only in certain postcolonial states, such as in the period designations "colonial architecture" or "colonial furniture." These two views of colonialism are reflected in the OED definition of the word "colonialism": "The colonial system or principle. Now freq. used in the derogatory sense of an alleged policy of exploitation of backward or weak peoples by a large power." The second part of this definition embraces a colonialist attitude in the definition of certain peoples as "backward" (compare the contemporary official designation in India of "other backward classes," OBCs, tellingly often referred to as "other backward castes").

If "colonization" refers to acts of settlement, "colonialism" can be defined as the system, practice, and principles of administration of colonies under colonial rule. Before the nineteenth century, colonization, even if authorized by the Crown, was for the most part spontaneous and relatively unregulated; by the mid-nineteenth century, governments sought to regularize the development of their colonies, and interested intellectuals produced theories of colonization. In general, colonizing countries did not employ the term "colonialism" for this, but simply used the more neutral word "colonization": in practice the two words cannot be completely distinguished. Even Aimé Césaire, in his outspoken denunciation of colonialism in *Discourse on Colonialism* (1950), criticizes "colonization" far more frequently than "colonialism." On the other side, in 1849 E. B. Wakefield published *A View of the Art of Colonisation* which suggested systematic principles for the management of the colonization of a colony, a theory that was then put into practice in New Zealand (and criticized by Marx in the last chapter of *Capital*). The most influential work proposing a theory and practice for the management of exploitation colonies was Lugard's *The Dual Mandate in British Tropical Africa* (1922), which advocated the principle of indirect rule, a mechanism that was in fact practiced throughout the empire.

Historically, colonization itself was rarely systematic, but by the late nineteenth century when the word "colonialism" was, according to the OED, first used in English (1886), colonial rule had become a system of sorts. Colonialism can be viewed in two fundamentally different ways – from the antithetical perspectives of the colonizer and of the colonized, or in the phraseology of James C. Scott (1998), between seeing like a state and seeing like a person in that state. For the colonial administrator, the colonial system would be thought of primarily in terms of the principles of colonial governance. These, as has been suggested, were very variable between and within different empires, but can nevertheless be seen to conform to certain fundamental paradigms of rule, direct or indirect, and law that were put into operation and supervised from the local capital, and overseen from the imperial center. To colonial administrators, the spectrum of colonies may have appeared to be very diverse – they were fond of arguing that their own colonial administration was very different (inevitably superior) from that of another imperial power. Even within the same empire, conditions in each colony were rarely the same: every one, in its own way, was a special case, with its own specific circumstances and problems. Nevertheless, all colonies within a single empire were recognizably part of an overall administrative system. Emphasis on the particularity of each colony or colonial system does not, however, mean that we cannot talk about colonialism in general, which always involves the subjugation of one people by another people whose own homeland is or was elsewhere. This common structural feature meant that all colonial administrators had to deal with the same problem: the native.

The other way of viewing the colonial system was through the eyes of that native, of those living under foreign rule. "All colonized people have much in common," remarks the Tunisian novelist Albert Memmi (Memmi 1967: ix): however different colonies may have seemed to the colonizers, to the colonized person the lived experience of one colonial domination would not have seemed very different from another, whether in terms of official status (India only became a colony in 1867, Ireland was technically never a colony) or a change from one imperial ruler to another. When there was a transfer of regime, they might prefer one or the other, as the Indonesians initially welcomed the Japanese in 1942 until they found themselves *romusha*, or as the Somalians preferred the Italians to the British in 1949, but whatever the regime, they remained colonized people without fundamental rights. It was this commonality of the colonized that encouraged anticolonial activists to establish international contacts with each other, and to learn from each other in terms of possible forms of anticolonial resistance. Whether in Africa, the Caribbean, South Asia, Southeast Asia, Australasia, Micronesia, Melanesia, or Polynesia, they were all in the same boat. Whatever it might be called, whatever its political designation, if a territory feels like a colony to the majority of its inhabitants, if they sense that they are dominated by an external power and have inadequate rights of representation, that they are considered racially or otherwise inferior people, then that makes it a colony to them.

For this reason, the term "internal colonialism" is often used when a minority, differentiated on grounds of religion, ethnicity, language, or region, considers that it is ruled by a majority in a quasi-colonial way. Internal colonialism designates the maintenance of inequality through political means: this difference will typically involve economic disparity (or "uneven development"), exacerbated by a perceived appropriation of resources, and a correlative lack of access to political power. Some writers such as Nicholas Thomas (1994) extend this situation to the conditions of modernity itself; others link it to larger analyses of unequal global economic formations such as Dependency or World Systems theory (Wallerstein 2004). The first use of the term "internal colonialism" was made in 1957 with reference to South Africa under the apartheid system, when a small white minority ruled over an African majority (Marquard 1957): as part of the complete social and political differentiation on grounds of race, Africans were not allowed to own land, and millions were forcibly evicted to specially created "homelands" or Bantustans, with which in fact most had no previous connection. The ultimate aim was that the Bantustans should become independent so that the African majority would no longer be citizens of South Africa: the internal colony was an example of what Adi Ophir has called, in relation to the occupied Palestinian territories, "inclusive exclusion" (Ophir et al. 2009). Other examples of internal colonialism would be Sardinia and the South of Italy (an issue known within Italy since the nineteenth century as the Southern Question), the treatment of the Tamil minority in Sri Lanka which led to the civil war of 1983–2009, the indigenous Maya people in Mexico (leading to the Zapatista rebellion which has been going on in different forms since 1994), and indeed arguably of indigenous peoples in many other countries around the world. By extension, the term is also sometimes used for regions where a sense of separate or distinct identity produces a demand for political autonomy, such as Catalonia in Spain or Scotland in the United Kingdom.

However different individual colonies may have been under formal colonial rule, as Jean-Paul Sartre argued in his essay "Colonialism is a System" (Sartre 2001), and Frantz Fanon in *The Wretched of the Earth* (Fanon 1966), colonialism always involved a racialized system of domination and exploitation through violence. Whether settler or exploitation colony, in terms of the mechanics of colonial rule, or the discursive regime that was developed to present and rule the colony, or the practices of enforcement, there was always an apparatus, already employed for other colonies, that would be put in place. This method can be analyzed historically and theoretically, just as it could be scrutinized critically by the people who fell under its regime of domination. For colonialism was a system of authority that constituted an objective practice of rule but also a regime of power that was felt as a subjective experience by colonized people. It is the coloniality, the colonial character or quality, of power and power structures that creates a bridge between the past and the present. There may be relatively few colonies today, but the experience of domination – political, military, economic, cultural – continues unbroken and is still felt by many peoples around the world, stirring feelings of resentment and producing formations and acts of resistance.

Critical analysis of "colonialism" will generally therefore come from the side of the colonized or from those who are taking their side, changing the perspective of colonization from that of the colonizers to that of those subjected to their rule, a shift in point of view that is reflected in the different resonances between "colonization" and "colonialism." Point of view also accounts for the use of "colonialism" in preference to "imperialism." In general, unless they were employing the discourse of communism or Marxism which criticized the capitalist system for the use of a global imperialism to serve its own ends, the colonized themselves were less focused on the empire as a whole than on their own colonial homeland. Historically, resistance to empire by the colonized typically came from within the colony, on a colony-by-colony basis, rather than from the empire as a whole. Although colonized people may have been against empire in general, their immediate political objective was generally focused on the colonial status of their own territory. To the colonized, it is well known that in each empire colonies can be added, and colonies can be lost. You do not need to destroy the empire as a whole to free yourself. From the imperial perspective, the perspective of the metropolitan center, the worry was that if one colony achieved its freedom, then all the others would want to follow suit.

The differing perspectives of metropole and colony are also reflected in the academic representation of historical colonialism. Broadly speaking, some western historians such as the Scottish historian Niall Ferguson (2002) continue to consider empire from the perspective of the imperial center, arguing for its positive virtues, while postcolonial or subaltern historians, such as the Indian historian Ranajit Guha (1997), write from the perspective of the colonized. The fundamental colonizer–colonized division continues to account for the difference between them.

As we have already seen in chapter 3, however, and as Memmi concedes in his *The Colonizer and The Colonized* (1967), while the colonizer–colonized antithesis offers the basic structure that operates between the people who live on two sides of the line of the power divide within the colony, it is, inevitably, too simplistic a schema: in practice, some people move across and between the line. Memmi himself distinguishes between the colonial administrators and what he calls the "small colonists," the relatively poor settler farmers who often came from impoverished countries elsewhere, such as Italy or Malta. Memmi also suggests that as a Tunisian Jew rather than a member of the Muslim majority in colonial Tunisia, he belonged to both sides, identifying with the French even while his social and political status was merely "one small notch above the Moslem on the pyramid which is the basis of all colonial societies." At once colonizer and colonized, both and neither, the Jewish population lived "in painful and constant ambiguity" (Memmi 1967: xiv, xxi, 15). Similarly, as Mahatma Gandhi argued in his 1909 nationalist manifesto *Hind Swaraj* (Gandhi 1997), many of the elite members of the colonized, such as lawyers or politicians, effectively behaved, or tried to behave, like the colonizers themselves, becoming, in V. S. Naipaul's phrase, "mimic men" (Naipaul 1967). The term *comprador* class is sometimes used to describe such people – today their equivalent would be the local class who serve as functionaries and interlocutors with international corporations and investors. Even the broader population may feel ambivalently toward the colonizer, at once admiring and hating them. The presence of such contradictory emotions meant that, as Homi K. Bhabha has argued, imitation could be as unnerving for the colonizer as overt hostility (Bhabha 1994: 85–92).

Imperialism

Although imperialism manifested itself as a practice, the meaning of the term was grounded in a political concept of expansive power, seeking to turn heterogeneous colonies into a single political and economic system. Imperialism necessarily involves empires, therefore, but all empires do not necessarily invoke imperialism. As with colony and colonialism, the meaning of empire and imperialism has shifted according to the political hegemony of their advocates or opponents. By the twenty-first century, the aura of both words has become irredeemably negative.

While the first British Empire was well established by the eighteenth century, despite the loss of the American colonies, the defeat of the French in India (1757) and then Canada (1763) prompted Napoleon Bonaparte's attempt to compensate for their loss by reinstituting a French empire through conquest of the European landmass. A new word was subsequently introduced to distinguish this "third way" of Napoleon's form of government between monarchy and republicanism, based on the model of the Roman Empire: *impérialisme* (1832). It was not, however, until the Second Empire of Napoleon III that the word traveled into English as "imperialism" (1858), in the course of which it moved from positive to negative: in English it was used as a way to describe the French political system of an autocratic emperor pursuing a policy of creating an empire not through trade or emigration, but the forcible appropriation of foreign territory through conquest (in the French case, consolidation of power in Algeria, invasions of or military missions to China, Cochinchina, Japan, the Levant, Mexico). Imperialism, the name by which the Napoleonic model of the French political system was known, was at this time actively rejected by British politicians and intellectuals as a form of despotism utterly alien to British traditions and to the dominant consensus at that time in favor of free trade. Within twenty years, however, the rebarbative French practice of imperialism was to be shamelessly translated into British policy by Benjamin Disraeli, whose second (but first substantial) term of office began in 1874. Ironically, it was in fact Gladstone, the liberal protector of the rights of indigenous people and the proponent of Home Rule in Ireland, who in practice expanded the British Empire more aggressively, for example, in Egypt. Although the negative marker associated with imperialism always endured for some oppositional figures such as Marx, in public discourse it gradually became more positive, associated with an imperialist policy of extending commerce through an actively acquisitive empire. As we shall see, whether there was really such a profound political distinction between imperialism and free trade as was argued at the time is open to doubt. While some radicals in Britain certainly advocated openly for the dismemberment of empire, in practice the British pursued their imperial interests by any means available, whether formal or informal.

These imports, exports, and insistence on the difference between the French and English words for imperialism were also indicators of what continued to be regarded as a significant variation in the political organization of empire. Toward the end of the century, British imperialism was conceived as a way of holding together an empire that at that time was seen by some as being at the point of dissolution – as Lenin notes in *Imperialism* (1965), even Disraeli at one point characterized the colonies as "millstones round our necks" – though as noted above, in practice imperialism continued apace throughout the nineteenth century; it just took different forms. The experience of the American War of Independence encouraged the British to organize their empire into units of largely autonomous dominions: the concept of a "Greater Britain" as a global confederation of Anglo-Saxon settler colonies, including for some (such as Cecil Rhodes) former colonies that were entirely independent such as the United States, was distinct from most other imperial powers in which imperialism involved the development of expansive concepts of "Greater France," "Greater Germany," "Greater Greece," "Greater Italy," or the "Greater Japanese Empire" (compare also Revisionist Zionism's "Greater Israel," which forms the basis of current settlement policy in the West Bank) – in which the colonial territories were integrated administratively into the metropolitan mainland and considered as an integral part of the sovereign state (Bell 2009; Young 2001, 2008). The modern Commonwealth of Nations, which includes a third of the world's population, comprises the major institutional legacy of Britain's organization of its empire on what might be anachronistically called self-deconstructing principles. In practice, however, there was always a contradiction between the settler colonies of the British Empire that were encouraged to become autonomous, and the exploitation colonies whose claims for autonomy were long resisted on grounds of racial inferiority. The different parts of the empire were run on entirely different principles, according to whether they were white or black.

With the entry of Germany, Italy, the United States, and Japan into the imperial game, imperialism became a form of power politics at the global level. By the last quarter of the nineteenth century, imperialism had become the dominant world political system, an era best symbolized by the 1884 Berlin conference in which the remaining territory of Africa, and also, though less well known, the Pacific, was divided up between the European nations by agreement between representatives of Austria-Hungary, Belgium, Denmark, France, the United Kingdom, Italy, the Netherlands, Portugal, Russia, Spain, Sweden-Norway, and the Ottoman Empire (the United States was invited, but somewhat surprisingly did not attend). While empire can describe a merely administrative arrangement for the government of diverse and diversely acquired territories, imperialism came to designate an ideology of empire which founded the identity of the originating imperial state, and whose interests lay in the circulation of trade (importing raw commodities from imperial possessions and re-exporting them as manufactured goods), increasing territorial control and maintaining autonomy from the threat of other empires. Ideological justifications for empire were generally added to these material and economic objectives – the *mission civilisatrice* (France), the rule of law (Britain), and racial superiority (all European empires).

At the height of European imperial power, however, imperialism came under attack not only through resistance across the empire itself, but also from liberal and left-wing thinkers within Europe. Along with J. A. Hobson's *Imperialism* (1902) and Nikolai Bukharin's *Imperialism and the Accumulation of Capital* (1924), the most famous of these was Lenin's *Imperialism: The Highest Stage of Capitalism* (1917), which decisively transformed the public meaning of imperialism from positive back to negative once more, even in France. Ever since, "imperialism" and "imperialist" have functioned as words of critique or abuse. Empire has been largely disavowed by states or politicians, and for the most part discussed in terms of something to be resisted and overcome (compare Mao Zedong's "US imperialism is a paper tiger" of July 14, 1956). Marxist theories of imperialism have been the most critical, the most incisive, and the most outspoken, continuously developing from Lenin to more recent examples such as Michael Hardt and Antonio Negri's *Empire*, published almost a century later (2000). In every case the basic presupposition remains the same as Lenin's, namely that modern empire is a form or product of capitalism which only seeks its own self-perpetuation and enrichment.

While this was the persuasive position on the left, for some conserva-
tive thinkers in Lenin's day, imperialism seemed to offer a means of
resistance to the development of industrialization and commercialization within the home state; as in the novels of Rider Haggard, or the
nomadic aestheticism of primitivists such as Paul Gauguin, the empire
offered a means of escape and a return to a rural alternative, as well as,
for some, an old-fashioned aristocratic lifestyle that would not have
been sustainable at home. It would be too simplistic therefore to see
imperialism merely as a way of enforcing national economic interests:
according to Davis and Huttenback (1986), the British Empire was in
practice a mechanism for transferring wealth from the middle to the
upper classes within Britain, while empire in its late phase increasingly
went against any purely financial advantage as imperial powers annexed
unprofitable territories simply so that a rival would not take them.
Imperial administrators might have gone as far as wishing to protect
current economic concerns, but at the same time they were often
actively resistant to innovations in practices of trade or industrialization
and preferred a state of what would later be called "underdevelopment" –
a precarious situation from which the postcolonial nation then had to
start out from. Indeed, the divorce between the empire and economic
return was one reason (along with the ever increasing cost of imperial
policing) why empires became progressively more uneconomic, expensive to maintain, and unsustainable (Hobsbawm 1985, 1987). Adam
Smith's critique of the monopoly companies that ran the British Empire
on the grounds of their inefficiency, which had led to their abolition
and the promulgation of the doctrine of free trade in the nineteenth
century, found itself once again relevant. One answer to the growing
cost of empire that emerged in the 1920s, and continues in a modified
form to this day in the idea of "overseas aid," was the idea of "development"
or "mise en valeur" – the novel notion that the role of the colonial power
was to support projects that would assist the local economy to grow.
Initially this was effected by setting up infrastructure and encouraging
exploitation of natural resources and industrialization by private
enterprise, but in later years colonial bureaucrats and economists moved
to planning and direct investment by the colonial government in areas
that included social welfare and ecology. Whereas earlier analysts, such
as Benjamin Kidd (1898), had considered tropical countries only in

terms of the commodities that they made available to Europe and the United States, from the 1930s economists saw the advantages of the colonies developing their own economies by increasing their productivity and therefore becoming less of a drain on imperial resources (Meredith and Havinden 2002; Hansen and Jonsson 2013).

Imperialism without Colonies

In response to the cost and the increasing impracticality of empire, around the end of the nineteenth century a different and more efficient kind of imperialism emerged that reestablished unashamedly economic priorities. As mentioned in the introduction to this chapter, whereas imperialism originally meant conquest and military occupation, directed from the center, by the end of the nineteenth century a new meaning had developed in which imperialism was linked to economic power reinforced by military strength, diplomatic pressure, and cultural influence, without necessarily involving territorial acquisition and physical occupation. This second kind of imperialism, of imperialism without colonies, was and still is often used in relation to the United States, and is associated with US policy in the Caribbean and South America. Although the United States began to acquire colonies in the Pacific from the mid-nineteenth century, it found that, having established South America as its sphere of influence with the Monroe Doctrine, it was able to exert economic pressure through trade alone. This gave it a financial and political advantage that was more effective than colonial occupation, and much cheaper to administer. "American" imperialism was achieved in part through what was known as "dollar diplomacy," exerting influence on a country through direct investment of capital and loans. Historians of the British Empire have developed a related concept of "informal empire" to describe the way in which the extent of British power, at its height, cannot simply be measured by the amount of territory colored red on the world map. Many nominally independent countries, from China to Afghanistan to the Trucial States (the modern Gulf States), were effectively run by the British through a combination of military power, financial muscle, and diplomatic pressure. At the same time, other regions, particularly in South America, fell under informal British control as a result of British financial interests in what has also been characterized as "free-trade imperialism": many of the most substantial and profitable British investments overseas in the nineteenth century were made in postcolonial independent South America, not in its own colonies (Gallagher and Robinson 1953). The German jurist and philosopher Carl Schmitt subsequently argued that this new system of imperialism was consolidated in the Treaty of Versailles of 1919, after which the era of European domination of the world beyond its borders that had obtained since 1492 was replaced by the Anglo-Saxon imperialism of the United States and Great Britain. Their informal imperialism was achieved through protectorates and financial controls consolidated by an unlimited "right of intervention," and supported by the concept of a "just war" that was written into the war-guilt clause (231) of the Versailles Treaty (Schmitt 2003: 13).

At the other end of the political spectrum, the new form of American imperialism, or British informal imperialism, was also the object of Lenin's 1917 critique in *Imperialism: The Highest Stage of Capitalism*: instead of exporting goods, he wrote, modern capitalism exports capital itself, producing "financial and diplomatic dependence, accompanied by political independence" (Lenin 1965: 102). Following Hobson, Lenin made the connection between imperialism and finance capitalism so that imperialism and capitalism have since become almost synonymous in left-wing discourse, where critical analyses of empire usually begin by establishing their ground in economic critique. Lenin's argument was that the conjunction of the two represented a particular form of imperialism and that modern imperialism was therefore not to be usefully compared to the parameters of the territorial expansion through conquest of historical empires in general. Imperialism, he argued, was a particular practice not so much of empires as of modern finance capitalism (for a non-Marxist version of imperialism as a form of "gentlemanly capitalism," see Cain and Hopkins 1993a, 1993b). Lenin's analysis laid the basis both for subsequent dependency theory and for the most influential Marxist theory of globalization, the core–semi-periphery–periphery model of world economies developed by World Systems theorists such as Immanuel Wallerstein (Wallerstein 2004). World Systems theory suggests that globalization comprises an economic hierarchy with dominant, semi-peripheral, and entirely peripheral economies. Globalization, like free-trade imperialism, is a competitive system of power.

In 1965, Kwame Nkrumah, President of newly independent Ghana, would characterize the practice of imperialism without colonies as "neo-colonialism – the last stage of imperialism" (Nkrumah 1965). Although the world system of empires has now passed away, the transmutation of imperialism into control by other means than direct territorial occupation explains why the term "imperialism" (or, after Nkrumah, "neo-colonialism") is still used to describe the political and military interventions and economic practices of powerful nations outside their territorial boundaries designed to maintain political and financial domination. The word is not, of course, much used by the powerful nations themselves, but rather by the disempowered who are experiencing domination by others: imperialism is always invoked as an object of resistance. In this sense, its use outside the West in the global South has not changed since the late nineteenth century. Apart from a brief flirtation with what some commentators claimed as the renewable possibilities of empire around the time of the invasion of Afghanistan in 2001, those in the West now generally disavow empire and imperialism, preferring the term "globalization."

6

Nation

The Nation as the Product of Colonial Expansion

"The expansion of Europe": the way that European colonialism and the growth of its empires used to be characterized implicitly suggests that "Europe" was an already constituted continent of nations which expanded its borders by acquiring colonial territories. This is far from the case. Europe developed into its current form through the process of amassing colonies: colonialism was a central element in the formation and construction of the European nation-states. It was a symbiotic process in which each formed a part of the other. Where chances of proximate physical expansion of individual countries were unavailable, colonies and the establishment of an overseas empire offered the same advantages as a larger land empire: increased trade, revenue, wealth, and power.

One of the distinctive features of European imperialism therefore was the seeming paradox that it was developed over the same time as the evolution of the democratic nation-state. The modern political form of the nation-state is usually held to have been formally initiated with the Treaty of Westphalia in 1648, a series of treaties that ended the Thirty Years War within the Holy Roman Empire and also officially confirmed the secession of the Dutch Republic from Spain. Implicitly, therefore, it acknowledged the principle of self-determination of nation-states. The

Empire, Colony, Postcolony, First Edition. Robert J. C. Young.
© 2015 Robert J. C. Young. Published 2015 by John Wiley & Sons, Ltd.

treaty remains important because it recognized within international law the existence of sovereign independent states outside the aegis of empire, and instigated the principle not only of separate sovereignty and territorial integrity but also, as part of that, of non-interference in the domestic affairs of other states. As a result, we speak of "Westphalian sovereignty" to describe the international political system based on a world made up of individual nation-states, a world that did not really fully come into being at a global level until after World War II. "Westphalian sovereignty" provides a useful shorthand to describe the transformation of the world political system from a collection of empires in the sixteenth century to nation-states by the end of the twentieth.

While there are many arguments among historians and others about which country or people formed the first nation, the Treaty of Westphalia marks the advent of the sovereign nation-state in its modern legal form. At its secession from the Spanish Empire in 1648, Holland became the first nation-state; it was also the first example of the achievement of sovereignty by a former colony, predating that of the United States by over a century. The first nation-state was created though an act of decolonization. Holland had not, however, been a colony in a modern sense of a territory occupied by violence: it had become part of the Hapsburg Spanish Empire through dynastic marriage and inheritance. However, in 1658, soon after the 17 Provinces (as they were then known) were inherited by Philip II of Spain, the Protestant Dutch rebelled, declaring independence with the 1581 Act of Abjuration, though it would not be until 1648 that their independence and sovereignty would be recognized by Spain. Dutch resistance was a response to Philip II's attempted suppression of Protestantism. When Portugal closed its ports, and therefore its African and Asian trade, to the Dutch in solidarity with Spain, it encouraged the Dutch to develop their own trade with the East, and subsequently to appropriate Portugal's trading posts. The growth of the Dutch colonial empire, therefore, occurred as an intrinsic part of the Dutch fight for independence and sovereignty. Even before Hapsburg rule, the Dutch had been active maritime traders. The position of Amsterdam as one of the major hubs of European trade, providing access to capital, led to the development of banking, insurance, and the first stock market in the city. Already by 1590, the Dutch were trading in the Mediterranean and around the coast of Africa and Brazil in competition with the Portuguese. In 1598 they established their first trading post on what would become the Dutch Gold Coast, in today's Ghana, and began to attempt to commandeer Portuguese trading posts in Brazil and the East Indies. By the time of formal independence at the Treaty of Westphalia, the Netherlands was already a colonial power, largely through the operations of the Dutch India Company (Vereenigde Oost-indische Compagnie, VOC), a vast multinational corporation that, like the British East India Company founded two years earlier, replicated many of the powers of a conventional state, such as possessing an army and navy. By means of the VOC, the Dutch set up, or seized from the Portuguese, trading posts in India, Ceylon, Dutch East Indies (Indonesia), Taiwan, Mauritius, and Japan (for two hundred and fifteen years the Dutch were the only Europeans allowed to trade in Japan). Four years after Westphalia in 1652, the first Dutch fort was built at what became Cape Town to service the sea route to the Indies. In order to maintain food supplies, nine VOC men were released from their contracts to become free burghers, "boers," in order to start farming, and with them began the Dutch colonization of South Africa.

The development of the first European nation-state was therefore fundamentally linked both to its own achievement of independence and to its acquisition of a colonial empire even before formal independence. The history of the Netherlands illustrates the way in which, despite the idea of the nation as a coherent single people, one typical feature of the nation was that once created, it sought to absorb or acquire more territory beyond its boundaries. Many nation-states, from the Netherlands in the seventeenth century, to the United States in the eighteenth, to Italy in the nineteenth, developed their prosperity in this way, an advantage that was not open to later postcolonial nations in the twentieth century.

The political struggles within Europe meant that the colonies were always part of the conflicts within nation-states as well as between them. Restricted at home by the social structures of late feudalism, trade and colonies offered the opportunity for bourgeois non-aristocrats to advance themselves and grow rich. While the expanding Protestant Dutch bourgeois class was developing capitalism with all its energy and liber-tarianism, the equivalent class was learning to do the same in England; before long the English had become main rivals to the Dutch. Just as the Dutch Empire was developed as part of the process of its becoming a nation-state, so too in Britain and even France; in the nineteenth century it would be Germany and Italy. The nationalist project of the unification of Italy involved freeing its provinces from the control of various empires and kingdoms, the last of which was from the Austro-Hungarian Empire which was dissolved in 1918; by 1918, however, the Italian nation had already created the Italian Empire by seizing Eritrea, Somalia, Libya, and the Dodecanese Islands (now part of Greece).

Historically, therefore, although this is not part of its mythology, colonialism was central to the development of the nation-state. That the first modern state had itself been a colony, in other words, was no aberration; it also points to the long-term logic of maritime colonization that was already apparent by the eighteenth century: that in time, colonies would want to become nations themselves. The nation as a political institution was historically inseparable from decolonization from empire and at the same time the advance of European global colonization. The eventual decolonization of the European maritime empires only reflects the evolution of this paradoxical logic by which nation-states emerged from empires only promptly to create new ones for themselves. Only after 1945 was the chain broken, so that (for the most part) nations no longer regarded the acquisition of an empire as an essential feature of the creation of a successful nation-state. Attention was turned instead to the newly invented concept of something that, like its own culture and just as much an imaginative creation, every nation needed for its success: an "economy" (Mitchell 2002: 4). The first gross domestic product (GDP) was calculated for President Roosevelt in 1942 (Coyle 2014). However, the legacy of the earlier logic lives on in the many border disputes, appropriations of territory and the like, that continue around the world (since 1947, India, for example, has annexed Kashmir, Hyderabad, Sikkim, Goa, Daman, and Diu; since 1967, Israel has occupied the West Bank and the Gaza strip, and annexed East Jerusalem and the Golan Heights; in 2014 Russia annexed Crimea; the full list of annexations and border disputes is a lengthy one). The imbrication of colony with nation meant that they developed as inseparable if antithetical entities.

Today, in a different way, the nation is often also a colony. For the "unalienable right" of a people to sever its contract with the sovereign does not work so easily when that people are part of a larger entity that takes the form of a single state rather than an empire. Historically the nation-state has often been formed by the aggregation of adjacent territories and has usually sought to integrate them into a homogeneous whole. It nevertheless frequently finds that certain regions, often geographically peripheral, begin to resist its power, sometimes making the claim that at a certain point in the past they had enjoyed their own autonomy or sovereignty and claiming that they are ruled through a form of internal colonialism. Think of the Southern states of the United States in the nineteenth century, of Scotland in Britain or Catalonia in Spain or Assam in India. From time to time reasonable states, or states encouraged to see reason, offer plebiscites. The twentieth century has in fact seen many of them, from that held in the Norwegian Union in 1905, to East Timor in 1999 (previously annexed by Indonesia). The Northern Ireland Good Friday agreement of 1998 was reached on the basis that if the majority of the population of Northern Ireland wishes to become part of Ireland, then it may do so. After a long and vociferous campaign for independence by Scottish nationalists, in a referendum held in 2014 a majority of Scotland's voting population turned out to decline the opportunity to secede from the United Kingdom. Independence movements by small nations that wish to secede from larger ones have been greatly facilitated in Europe by the existence of the larger political, quasi-federal body of the European Union. Most nation-states, however, reject the demands of sovereignty movements automatically. India, for example, still refuses to hold the plebiscite in Indian-administered Kashmir requested by the United Nations in 1948 after the Indian invasion of the previous year. Democratic India has preferred to fight intermittent wars with Pakistan rather than allow the Kashmiri people to determine their own political destiny.

The inconsistency with regard to forms of internal colonialism such as these emerges as the fundamental contradiction within international law with respect to the nation-state: on the one hand, it affirms the right to self-determination for all peoples, and yet on the other hand it affirms the territorial integrity of sovereign nation-states. As became clear in 2014 when Crimea and Southern and Eastern Ukraine sought to leave Ukraine in order to join the Russian Federation, the two simply do not add up.

The Nation and Human Rights

Anticolonial nationalism and Protestant capitalism were not the only elements at play in the creation of empire: France, for example, had been concerned since the time of Louis XIV to turn itself into a nation-state by creating a vertical, homogeneous culture of language and religion out of its heterogeneous peoples. As a part of this process, France developed imperial mercantile ambitions commensurate with those of Spain and Portugal. As early as 1534 the French established their first trading post in Quebec, though it was not properly colonized until 1605. The seventeenth century saw them founding a number of colonies in the Caribbean, including French Guiana, Guadeloupe, and Martinique. They also set up trading posts in Senegal and, rather late in the day compared to their competitors, in India from 1668. In the course of a succession of wars with the British in the eighteenth century, France lost almost all her extensive colonies in the Americas and India, one factor that contributed to the unrest that produced the French Revolution of 1789. The lost colonies determined the fate of the imperial state as much as the military failures of the imperial state determined the fate of the colonies.

It was, however, another lost colony that provided the model for the Republican nation-state to the French in 1789, leading to their radical act of self-Americanization. The declaration of independence and establishment of the United States through settler anticolonial revolution against British rule in 1776 created the second nation-state that had formerly been a colony, this time outside mainland Europe. Like the Dutch Act of Abjuration to which it may have been indebted, the Declaration of Independence began with a list of unredressed grievances that provided justification for the settlers' decision to declare the sovereignty of the ruler terminated. Asserting "unalienable rights" to be endowed by God to men, and claiming that if the social contract was broken, then the authority of the ruler may be justly removed, the Declaration of Independence provided the foundational precedent for all subsequent attempts to throw off oppressive rule by the people in any state, provoking what David Armitage has called "a contagion of sovereignty" (Armitage 2007: 103). How much more powerful that argument would become if there had never been any form of social contract or consent, if the ruler had installed himself within living or historical memory solely by force of arms, as in any exploitation colony. The birth of the idea of the nation as the institution whose function was to guarantee civil and human rights, as formulated by the American and French Declarations and subsequently by Thomas Paine in *The Rights of Man* (1791), was radical enough in Europe, but a complete threat to the government of the colonies. Small wonder that Paine's book was banned in British India: it has remained the most powerful political ideology of freedom in colonized and authoritarian countries right into the twenty-first century. With such political doctrines in the native armory, colonial rulers had their work cut out to justify their rule in other terms. Nevertheless, until the nineteenth century, most of the arguments against colonial rule expressed in print were made by colonists themselves: their anticolonialism, whether that of Thomas Jefferson, Wolfe Tone, or Simón Bolívar, was not against colonialism as such (after all, they were colonists themselves) but against the rule of the settler colony by the metropolitan government.

Though the development of human rights and anticolonialism are historically entwined, American anticolonialism was developed on very different premises from those that emerged later: Jefferson and Bhagat Singh would probably have had very little in common had they met. In claiming "unalienable rights" for the people, the US Declaration of Independence drew on the new political discourse of the eighteenth century which was organized according to the concept of rights. As Hannah Arendt argued in *The Origins of Totalitarianism* (Arendt 1958), the development of the idea of the nation-state itself occurred as part of the process of the development of the concepts of rights, not the other way round. In both the American Declaration of Independence of 1776, and the French Declaration of Rights of 1789, the argument begins with the claim that human beings (in fact, the contemporary generic term "men" was used) are born free and equal in rights, from which the French Declaration declares that it follows that the aim of every political association (that is, the nation) is then the preservation of these natural rights. As the American Declaration puts it, "to secure these rights, Governments are instituted among Men, deriving their just powers from the consent of the governed."[1] Conceptually in both declarations, therefore, the state is *nothing more* than that which secures the human rights of those within it. This civic conception of the nation is completely at odds with later ideas of nationalism in which the nation becomes the totality and expression of the culture or spirit of a particular ethnic group. In that respect, nationalism, the force that drove the creation of many nations, has queered the pitch of the nation which in a postcolonial world has often lost sight of its original function – to uphold the rights and freedom of all its citizens. In the context of critiques of coercive nationalist nation-states that were developed toward the end of the twentieth century, commentators have emphasized the utopian project of the nation on its republican basis as a civic institution that secures the rights of its citizens (Moyn 2010; Slaughter 2007). Contemporary human rights discourse is not just about the assertion of human rights, it forms part of an attempt to turn nations back into the guarantors rather than the violators of human rights, in a context in which the nation-state itself has lost much of its sovereign power, so that human rights have become an unenforceable international legal obligation of the nation-state. For this reason, Giorgio Agamben argues that the refugee, with no state to guarantee his or her rights, is more aptly the figure of our age than the citizen (Agamben 1998a).

The Nation, Human Rights, and Slavery

Enlightenment ideas emerged in conjunction with developments that were marshaled against the arbitrary and unrepresentative rule of colonial government by imperial powers. The French assertion of liberty followed the central defining feature of the American Revolution: the American founding fathers, in turn, held their doctrine of the inalienable right of liberty to be authorized by an older Anglo-Saxon right of liberty embodied in the English tradition of legal documents that tempered the arbitrary power of the king while establishing the rights of his subjects – the Magna Carta of 1215, the Petition of Right of 1628, and the Bill of Rights of 1689.[2] The French also emphasized the idea of equality and fraternity, which inevitably raised the whole issue of gender equality that would be highlighted by Mary Wollstonecraft. The immediate question, however, was what form the state should take that would guarantee the "unalienable rights" of its people. While the Dutch initially looked for an alternative sovereign, the American founding fathers located and locked authority in the nation itself: "we, the people." When France became a republic in 1792 a few years after that phrase was formulated in the American Constitution of 1789, it followed suit. Both the French and the legislators of the thirteen colonies were fortunate in that the geographical boundaries of their new states were not immediately at issue. What defined the state was the people, who in turn defined the nation. But what is a nation? And what or rather who exactly is a people? In a country with indigenous Native Americans and African slaves does "the people" include everyone? Is everyone a citizen? The Americans said no, the French yes – and then, a little later, no.

The American Revolution was founded on the idea of human liberty, but this attribute of humanity was not extended either to Native Americans or slaves. The founding fathers did not theorize this contradiction, but its conceptual logic operated at the basis of their argument: liberty was not for all humans, only for white European ones, or alternatively, liberty was for humans, but non-white people were not considered fully human. The contradiction was only formally resolved by the American Civil War of 1861–5, but its legacy continues to reverberate in the United States today. The same contradiction would haunt the colonies until their emancipation.

As we saw in chapter 4, the revolutions of the eighteenth century produced renewed public debates in Europe about the ethics of colonies and slavery. The French revolutionaries were quick to realize that their newly proclaimed rights of man were incompatible with their colonial practices. Soon after the onset of the French Revolution, the question began to be asked whether the principles of liberty, fraternity, and equality should include the remaining French colonies of Senegal and the Caribbean, and whether slavery was compatible with the principles of the French Revolution. Should liberty be extended to colonies and to the slaves in them, as the Englishman Jeremy Bentham advocated in his radical 1793 pamphlet, *Emancipate Your Colonies!*? Contradictory positions were taken on slavery: the Republican government freed the slaves in 1794, Napoleon then reenslaved them, or tried to (Dubois 2004). In the French colony of San Domingue (Haiti), the French Revolution immediately produced demands for civil rights from the people of color and slaves. In 1791 the slaves themselves broke out into open rebellion, and though the French made several attempts to reestablish control of the island they never succeeded in doing so. If the United States was the first settler colony to revolt against its colonial status, then, as C. L. R. James was to emphasize in 1938 in *The Black Jacobins* (James 2001), Haiti was the first colony in which slaves and people of color successfully revolted against both the settlers and the colonial government. In both cases, the colonies achieved freedom through violent rebellion, justifying their actions through the principles of the rights of man.

How far, though, was the language of rights itself determined by the practice of slavery? Paul Gilroy has argued that discussion of the genealogy of human rights has ignored the context of slavery and colonialism in which it was developed, and the debates "over who could qualify for recognition as a rights-bearing subject in a right-bearing body." He continues: "This orientation necessitates a genealogy for human rights that differs from the usual one. It should begin with the history of conquest and expansion, and must be able to encompass the debates over how colonies and slave plantations were to be administered" (Gilroy 2010: 57).

More recently, Peter de Bolla has shown how, in the language of the American colonists, one of the arguments against British despotism was that it reduced the colonists to a state of slavery: if we are deprived of our liberty, then we are nothing better than our slaves! (de Bolla 2014: 131–205). Their own slave society, in other words, was the context from which American colonists developed their discourse of liberty and freedom for themselves.

Human rights talk, rights based on a concept of freedom, and the nation-state as the guarantor of the rights of humankind, were developed and defined in the Enlightenment within the framework of increasing debates about the morality of slavery that had begun in the seventeenth century; it thus emerged directly from the conditions of global European colonization with slavery as its defining institution. The patriotic refrain of James Thomson's "Rule Britannia" (1740), "Britons never shall be slaves," echoed in the line "as freemen not slaves" in the actor David Garrick's equally patriotic "Heart of Oak" (1760), encapsulates the way in which the discourse of liberty and associated human rights in the eighteenth century were defined directly against the slave societies that Europeans had themselves created. This leads to the following formulation: the nation embodies a political configuration that guarantees that you should not be the slave of another. It was therefore only logical that in time those whom Europeans had enslaved, or colonized, should also seek their own nation in order to guarantee human rights for themselves too.

Notes

1 http://www.archives.gov/exhibits/charters/declaration_transcript.html.

2 It is sometimes claimed that the Persian Cyrus cylinder in the British Museum, dating from the sixth century BCE, constitutes the earliest document of human rights; however, there is little in the inscription that corroborates this view.

7

Nationalism

The idea of nationalism is one of the most generally misunderstood in the modern world. The Imperialists do not even try to understand it; they simply call it sedition and hand it over to the police. (Robert Wilson Lynd, 1911)

For nineteenth-century empires, nationalism and democracy were words as subversive and threatening as communism in the twentieth. For colonized people, nationalism was what bound them together in opposition to the colonizer. Ironically, the idea had been invented in Europe, but that did not bother anyone until afterwards. (Partha Chatterjee 1986)

The problem for any aspiring nation under the rule of an alien power is that if the external authority is illegitimate, then where does legitimate authority lie? There were two possible answers to this question, once the divine right of kings was no longer considered credible: either the deposed local or national ruler or his or her descendants, assuming that such a person had previously been the ruler of the same territory that became the colony, or a new constituency, inspired by the republican revolutions of America and France: the people. The question, however, especially for a colony whose territorial boundaries had been often arbitrarily constructed, was then who are its people? Are the indigenous or

Empire, Colony, Postcolony, First Edition. Robert J. C. Young.
© 2015 Robert J. C. Young. Published 2015 by John Wiley & Sons, Ltd.

native inhabitants of the colony "a people" in a political sense? If not, how might they become one?

The nation as defined through the French Revolution transformed the way that populations thought about the political formations in which they lived. If the answer to the question of who was the nation was the people, then what made them a people in the sense of one specific people, a cohesive group, rather than a diverse population? Can an assorted population be "a people?" In France, the earlier French centralization of the state, and the demand for linguistic and religious uniformity, had provided one answer to this question – indeed the republican idea of the nation was in one sense a product of it, though that had not been the way that Louis XIV had envisaged it. Moreover a nation does not simply exist like an object: even after the Revolution the French nation has had to be continuously reconstructed to maintain a sense of its own identity. It is not so much that there are "natural" nations that are already in existence and ones that have to be constructed, as that all nations are constructed – only the historical moment when they become a nation or a nation-state varies. Arguably many states have never become "nations," just as many nations, such as the Kurds or the Palestinians, have not yet become states, although it is arguably the struggle for statehood that has made them a nation. Many colonies or protectorates became states before they developed into nations: for example, the people of the United Arab Emirates did not think of themselves as a nation until the arrangements for independence were negotiated and those emirates that were going to join the UAE were agreed upon. An independent state of this kind then begins the process of "nation building," which means trying to make the inhabitants feel as if they are a part of and belong to a nation. No nation was simply always there in the first place – they all have to be imagined (Anderson 1983). It is just a question of whether this takes place before or after they become a state, whether a people are looking for a state, or a state is looking for a people (Hobsbawm 1990).

This description passes over an important difference between the emergence of the first and later nation-states. A nation-state can be conceived in terms of a civic or ethnic identity. As we have seen, for the French or American revolutionaries, the state was less a nation as such than the secular political institution developed by the people for the people which guaranteed their human and civil rights. Their loyalty to the state followed as its citizens. They could think in this way because the state was in some sense already in existence – it was a question of rearranging it from a despotic to a democratic formation. But what if, as in the case of Germany at the end of the eighteenth century, there was no state that corresponded to any concept of the German people? It was this situation that required the creation of something that was virtually absent at the time of the American Revolution: nationalism. Nationalism, as it developed, was in many respects at odds with the original conception of the nation-state. Instead of being the guarantor of human and civil rights, this kind of nation was agitated for, and then created, on the basis of similarity. That similarity could take the form of a shared language, religion, history, culture, or racial or ethnic identity – or all or some of these. Nationalism was designed to make people feel as though they belonged together, and produce the demand for political autonomy. The issue of human rights was largely absent other than as the one right of self-determination. Nationalism therefore tends toward the very opposite end of the political spectrum from the liberal republicanism of the United States and France. For with cultural identification comes the demand for homogeneity, which produces not individual rights but the requirement for the individual to conform to the characteristics of the group, that is the state – with an identifiable, uniform language, religion, culture, or race. In the program of Shiv Senna in India, for example, the homogenization of the nation is determined on religious grounds: their dream of an allegedly once "pure" Hindu India means removing traces not only of the last invaders, the British, but the ones before that, the Mughals (but not the ones before that). In practice, this encourages the prejudice and violence against Muslims that was evident in the Gujarat massacres of 2002, as well perhaps as accounting for the frequency with which you see Hitler's *Mein Kampf* on pavement bookstalls on the streets of India. As a result, nationalist nations exist at the other end of the spectrum from civic nation-states, which is in fact the model under which India was set up. The concept of the nation-state therefore accommodates two very different political forms: the secular, in which the nation acts as the neutral guarantor of civil rights, and the cultural, in which the nation is identified with a specific group with a common identity.

While it was the Americans and French who created the first nation-state of which the people were sovereign, it was the Germans who first developed a fully theorized concept of what the nation-state should be for those with a common identity. At that time, at the end of the eighteenth century, Europe contained people whom we would now call Czechs, Germans, Hungarians, Poles, Russians, Slovaks, and many others, none of whom had a country of their own: aside from France, the continent was still governed as a set of empires. The territory of modern Germany formed part of the Holy Roman Empire, which by 1700 was under the nominal control of the Hapsburg monarchy but divided into hundreds of independent principalities, of which the largest and most powerful was Prussia. The Holy Roman Empire was abolished after the Napoleonic invasion of 1803, but it was not until 1871 that the heterogeneous North German Confederation was united into the German Empire under the initiative of Bismarck's Prussia. The problem for any concept of Germany as a nation was that it had no natural geographic boundaries of the kind that were available to Britain, France, or Spain. The flat lands of the German plains stretch all the way to the Russian steppes. Moreover, as a result of a range of historical factors, the German people were themselves spread over much of Eastern Europe, in cities now located in modern Russia (Kant's Königsberg is now Kalingrad), the Czech Republic, Poland, Romania, and elsewhere – Prussia alone contained territories that are now part of modern Belgium, the Czech Republic, Denmark, Lithuania, Poland, Russia, and Switzerland. German was spoken in a large variety of almost mutually incomprehensible forms, together with "low" forms of German such as Dutch/Flemish. Even religion did not bring them together, rather the reverse in fact: although Luther, a German, had initiated Protestantism, Germans further south remained Catholic; the two sides had fought against each other in the ruinous Thirty Years War of 1618–48.

The philosopher Johann Gottfried Herder, himself a Prussian, was the first philosopher to develop a political philosophy oriented toward developing a national identity for Germany as a nation of a particular people that could solve the problem of a religious divide and scattered, undefined territory (Barnard 2003). Herder began by redefining the people not as a group who possessed certain natural rights, as had been the case for the Americans and the French, but as a *volk*, a folk. What made a particular set of people an identifiable *volk*? Herder's answer was a revolutionary concept that would transform our conception of our lives right up to the present: a culture. Herder invented the idea of a "culture" in order to create the nation; the two have been inextricably intertwined ever since. His concept of culture was designed to identify the commonality that certain people share with respect to their whole way of life: above all, a common language. An individual language, according to Herder, anticipating what would later be called the Sapir–Whorf hypothesis, mediates the way people conceptualize the world, it makes them see the world according to particular perceptions and values (a simple example would be the way that languages do not all divide up the colors of the rainbow into the same distinct colors – some languages do not, for instance, distinguish between blue and green). Herder identified the specific culture of a people that developed in consonance with their language as the lore of the *volk*: folklore. Culture was identified with the day-to-day lives of ordinary folk, not just with the more cosmopolitan "art" of the elite, though that was by no means excluded. Culture was the culture of the people, "popular": the nation was its expression. What unites a people and makes them feel that they belong to one nation rather than another, Herder argued, was not their being subjects of a particular sovereign or state, but possessing a common life-world. Culture and nation became indissolubly identified at all levels, as they have been ever since. Think of the label placed beside a painting in any museum: after the name comes the artist's nationality – why is that so important?

The components that identified a nation, according to Herder, were its language and its popular culture, its folklore. Soon researchers such as the brothers Grimm started to collect German folk tales, fairy tales, popular ballads, popular music and dance forms. Before long, contemporary artists and musicians began to see their own work as contributing to the soft power that made a nation and started to integrate popular local forms into their work (in 1825 Chopin, for example, began to write piano music in the form of the traditional Polish folk dance, the Mazurka; soon the integration of folk songs into "classical" music became commonplace). Writers developed the novel form into the historical or metaphorical narrative of the nation, as in the work of Sir Walter Scott or Leo Tolstoy. The kind of art that they produced can be connected to the ways in which in the nineteenth century culture tended to be seen as working toward the presentation of harmony and forms of totality, just like the ideal of the nation-state itself. Some writers made the political connection explicitly, for example Matthew Arnold in *Culture and Anarchy* (1867–9), the principle point of which is to present culture and anarchy, by which Arnold meant liberalism, in other words, the Enlightenment philosophy of rights, of liberty and equality, as alternative choices for the state and the nation. It could have been called *Culture or Rights*. In the twentieth century, while in the colonial world culture continued to serve the anticolonial purposes of aspiring nations, in Europe and North America after World War I, artists broke away from this acquiescent and increasingly nationalistic political alliance to establish art as the activity which criticizes society and its norms, particularly its relation to instrumental capitalism, by presenting dissonance and fragmentation. This shift usually goes by the name of Modernism; its most articulate spokesperson in this respect is the German philosopher Theodor Adorno. Modernism's "international style" was a deliberate strategy to move beyond the service, and confines, of the nation.

In Germany, Herder's ideas were galvanized into a wider popularity by Napoleon's invasion of German territories and his (unsuccessful) attempt to impose the French language on the Germans. From the first, nationalism would develop above all as a reaction against colonial or imperial power which was seen as repressing the culture of a people, a common culture which in turn was considered to give its people the right to determine their own political existence. During the course of the nineteenth century a new component was added in Europe to solidify a sense of individual national solidarity, the idea of race. In the German case, the Teutonic origins of the Germans meant that racial theorists claimed that they formed a race distinct from all others. The logical corollary of this form of racialized thinking was that people, who in other respects might be culturally German, such as German Jews, were not really Germans. Such eventually became the extremity of Nazi thought, with its calamitous consequences. An analogous form of thinking applies to any nationalist ideology which proclaims a single identity based on one factor, rather than a shared culture. The idea of a single feature – race or religion – comprising national identity typically emerges as a potent part of the process of the struggle for the nation's formation, but usually does not become oppressive until later, when extremists attempt to consolidate power within the nation-state. Three nations created at around the same time in 1947–8 that have verged toward a single criterion of belonging – Israel, Pakistan, Sri Lanka – have also proved to be vectors of political instability (Devji 2013). The most successful nation-states have been those which, even if created on the basis of nationalist sentiment, have been able subsequently to turn toward the other inclusive model of the heterogeneous nation, that is, the civic – states such as Norway or Sweden, whose primary concern has been the welfare and upholding of the civil rights of all their citizens, as well as accepting international responsibility for others in need, particularly refugees and those in need of asylum.

As a political strategy for the creation of nation-states, nationalism, a shared popular culture, was the force that was identified and harnessed in order to create a common identity that would provide the basis for the political will among a collection of people to become a nation-state. The strategy has been extremely successful: historically, nothing apart from religion has created such a powerful group dynamics as much as nationalism. For better or for worse, people have been much more willing to identify with the ideas of nationalism than with communism and concepts of working-class solidarity. The contradiction, however, remains that such nationalism has rarely been subsequently put into the service of the interests of the people as a whole. It has rather been used by the capitalist classes to break up existing social structures (whether of local or colonial empires) in order to develop and consolidate their own economic interests and power. This explains the otherwise apparent contradiction in India of the nationalist, traditionalist BJP being simultaneously the most hospitable party to international business and neoliberal economic policy.

The nation-state was developed in Europe by means of colonial expansion, but it was also, as has been argued, established from the first through resistance to imperial power. Empires and nations exist in direct antimony toward each other. It was only logical, therefore, that nationalism should have been the primary political movement to be set in motion in the colonies in order to resist European control. If Germans had provided the conceptual basis to create the motor of nationalism, it was also in Europe that the first great anti-imperial nationalist movements would emerge that demonstrated to others how it could be done: in Greece, in Italy, and in Ireland. Ireland provides a powerful example since, in the face of continuing failure to win independence, the Irish embarked upon both forms of nationalism, civic and cultural: the United Irishmen Rebellion of 1798 followed the American and French models, whereas the Young Ireland movement of the 1840s developed a cultural nationalism of a Germanic type. The Greek War of Independence, fought against the Ottoman Empire between 1821 and 1832, was the first successful anti-imperial nationalist movement waged on culturalist grounds. The result, ominously, was not only the formation of a new nation-state but also the first purification of a culture in which an attempt was made to eliminate all alleged foreign elements acquired since Classical times (St Clair 1972; Mackridge 2009). In encouraging nationalist movements within the Ottoman Empire throughout the nineteenth and early twentieth centuries, European powers seem to have remained blithely oblivious of the fact that they were creating the mechanisms of the dissolution of their own empires. They persisted in the delusional belief that somehow the "Oriental" Ottoman Empire was constitutively different from their own.

8

Anticolonialism

Perhaps Garibaldi could not have succeeded in mobilizing the army with such ease if Mazzini had not invested his thirty years in his mission of cultural and literary renaissance. The revival of Irish language was attempted with the same enthusiasm along with the renaissance in Ireland. The rulers so much wanted to suppress their language for the ultimate suppression of the Irish people that even kids were punished for the crime of keeping a few verses in Gaelic. The French Revolution would have been impossible without the literature of Rousseau and Voltaire. Had Tolstoy, Karl Marx, and Maxim Gorky not invested years of their lives in the creation of a new literature, the Russian Revolution would not have taken place, leave alone the propagation and practice of communism. (Bhagat Singh, "The Problem of Punjab's Language and Script," *1933)*

Anticolonialism

We can distinguish three ideologies of anticolonialism, each of which in turn operated according to two alternative practical strategies, reform and revolution. They developed in distinct historical phases. In the eighteenth century, anticolonialism was founded on ideas of natural law, liberty, and human rights; the dominant nineteenth-century mode,

Empire, Colony, Postcolony, First Edition. Robert J. C. Young.
© 2015 Robert J. C. Young. Published 2015 by John Wiley & Sons, Ltd.

whether in Greece, Ireland, or Italy, was based on sentiments of nationalism. In the twentieth century, particularly after 1917, such nationalism was assimilated with ideas of socialism and revolutionary communism. Each century brought its own organizing ideas of anticolonialism. Although there are many individual examples, such as the successful Mahdist revolt in the Sudan against Egyptian/British rule in 1883–5, religion was less often a major factor. That would be reserved for the twenty-first century.

Why anticolonialism rather than anti-imperialism? It depends where you are looking at the empire from. If you see it from the center, considering the whole system, then you might develop a critique of imperialism as communists such as Lenin did. On the other hand, each "possession" that had been brought under control of empire was a colony. Local resistance therefore focused for the main part on the colonial status of that territory rather than the whole system of which it formed a part.

Anticolonialism is as old as colonialism: it was hardly ever likely that those whose territories were arbitrarily annexed for colonial rule, whether by settlers or armies, would feel entirely content with the new arrangement. However, what indigenous people felt about themselves or the dispossession of their territories was rarely recorded before the nineteenth century (Pratt 1994). For the most part, during the history of empires, anticolonial sentiment was expressed simply, by means of rebellion and revolt. Though little may be known about the individuals or the circumstances, the history of revolt constitutes a precise record of opposition to empire and colonization, just as the history of slave revolts, which occurred almost annually in the Americas, forms a written testimony of slaves' active resistance against the barbarity of their condition (Blackburn 1988; Mishra 2012). Aside from those of the colonizers themselves in the Americas and South Africa in the first Boer War and the Greek War of Independence, and with the notable exception of Haiti, very few rebellions or revolts before the twentieth century were successful. Why was this? In the first place, it was a question of relative scale of military power. But the failure of rebellions was also conceptual: many rebels had not prepared strategically. The Indian rebellion of 1857 would be a case in point, and this was the lesson that Bhagat Singh understood in 1933. However spectacular its initial success, and though the rebellion spread spontaneously across central Northern India, there had been no long-term preparation, and no overall coordinated strategy and objective. It was put down by the British using Indian troops. Singh's emphasis on the importance of culture to revolution marks a significant shift in anticolonial politics in the twentieth century and suggests the extent to which it drew on successful European examples, particularly those of Italy, Russia, and Ireland. The Indian socialist understood the significance of Leninist revolutionary methods, while at the same time stressing the importance of sustained cultural preparation for achieving them. This was a lesson that was learnt by many anticolonial revolutionaries in his time and became a significant factor in their eventual success: spontaneity was not to be relied upon.

Anticolonial revolution in the Americas was victorious in the late eighteenth and early nineteenth centuries because it was well organized and because the people involved had absorbed a set of revolutionary ideas that held them together and gave them clear political objectives. They were also, for the most part, popular revolutions – among the settlers. Effective anticolonial revolution needs to operate from below. When the majority of the local population, men and women, supports rebellion, the local leaders become powerful and the colonizer becomes powerless. This was the great lesson taught above all by European nationalism. For most anticolonial activists, therefore, the primary form of anticolonialism was as much cultural as political: to develop ideas that would shift sentiments of colonized people from acquiescence to rebellion. By far the most effective way to do that was to build up nationalist sentiment, which by definition meant through culture.

The fact that all early examples of anticolonial movements occurred either in European settler colonies in the Americas or in Europe itself, correlates with the fact that moral and political objections to European colonial rule were also made from the earliest days of imperial expansion by Europeans themselves, from Bartolomé de las Casas in the sixteenth century, to Jonathan Swift and Aphra Behn in the seventeenth, to Edmund Burke, Jeremy Bentham, Denis Diderot, and Voltaire in the eighteenth, to Karl Marx and Goldwin Smith in the nineteenth, to W. E. B. Dubois, Lenin, Sylvia Pankhurst, and many others in the twentieth (Merle 1969). As was discussed in chapter 4, resistance to empire formed an intrinsic part of the development of the ideas of the nation, liberty, representative government, and self-determination, all of which contradicted the practice of colonies and empire. The Irish political philosopher Edmund Burke is most associated with the view that autocracy abroad was also dangerous because it corrupted liberty at home, and that colonial rule was properly a matter of trusteeship for indigenous people. Liberal concern for the treatment of natives – the Spanish Crown had already passed legislation about the treatment of Native Americans by 1512–13 – may have served to make European empires somewhat more ethical in governance (which is not to say that this was widely observed, especially by settlers), and may account for some of the marked differences between the severity of rule in European and Japanese colonies (Heartfield 2011). Not unconnected to ideas of aboriginal "protection," resistance to empire was also encouraged by the simultaneous growth of human rights movements, particularly the anti-slavery movement, whose ethics would apply equally to colonial subjects, and provided a moral and political opposition to the domination and subordination structure of empire. These concerns contributed to the establishment of international law, ideas of justice, and norms of ethical behavior within a system of global governance. Initially, therefore, it was Europeans who typically objected to imperial rule in general: indigenous people, seeing things from the perspective of their homeland, were more likely to protest politically against the specific rule of their own country as a colony.

Anticolonial Nationalism: Italy and Ireland

While the American revolutions in North and South America were the founding anticolonial revolutions in the modern era, they did not provide an easy example to follow for those living in Africa or Asia. It is noticeable that with a few exceptions, such as the Vietnamese declaration of independence in 1945, by the twentieth century, few non-European anticolonialists referred back to the American–French tradition in their arguments. The claims for human rights, liberty, and democracy, though by no means discarded, lacked emotional appeal at that point, and appeared to have been superseded by the rival promises of nationalism, socialist equality, and the identification of the colonizer with capitalist exploitation. Socialism, too, would always remain comparatively cerebral: the great example of anticolonial revolution, which inspired all colonized peoples, was the Italian Risorgimento. As Singh observed, Italian unification was conceived of as much more than just the establishment of the political unity of Italy. It was also an idealistic, nationalist movement involving a rebirth, a renaissance of Italy, Italian culture, the Italian people, of Italianness altogether. Its spectacular moments caught the imagination of the world and became the template of anticolonial revolution. By 1848 the Risorgimento had become a popular cause enthusiastically endorsed by ordinary Italian people across the still-fragmented states of Italy: nationalism was something with which almost everyone could identify. As the Reader puts it in Gandhi's primer for self-rule, *Hind Swaraj* (1909): "What was possible for Mazzini and Garibaldi is possible for us" (Gandhi 1997: 72).

After 1815, "Italy" had been reconfigured in parts, variously as a group of individual kingdoms, duchies, the papal state, and the kingdom of Venetia, which was part of the Austro-Hungarian Empire. Italian reunification was not strictly, then, an anticolonial war, but it was the triumph of nationalism against feudal and imperial states that made it the template of anticolonial modernity. The dynamic leader Giuseppe Garibaldi provided a direct link between revolutionary military campaigns for republics in Brazil and Uruguay in South America and the nationalist uprisings in Italy of 1848. His military prowess and intense popularity among Italians were augmented by his abilities to play off external powers against each other and draw on the assistance of others, for example the British, when needed. His success was only tempered by political complications and differences between the leaders of the Risorgimento, such as whether Italy should become a monarchy or republic. While Garibaldi had extraordinary military skill and immense charisma, Giuseppe Mazzini developed the revolutionary ideological impetus by forming La Giovine Italia (Young Italy) while in exile in Marseilles, a political movement whose name embodied the idea of rebirth. It was subsequently imitated all over the world by anticolonial activists as a means of providing the basis for a cultural and political kernel that would empower revolution (for example, Young Ireland, organized by Thomas Davis, or *Young India*, a newspaper published by Gandhi; the Arch Duke Franz Ferdinand was assassinated in Sarajevo in 1914 by a member of the revolutionary nationalist Mlada Bosna, "Young Bosnia," movement). While Mazzini worked at times alongside Garibaldi, both of them strong believers in popular democracy, the third figure of the Risorgimento, Camillo Benso Cavour, was very different. He was a pragmatic politician who preferred diplomatic initiatives at the highest level to popular politics. As Prime Minister of the Kingdom of Piedmont-Sardinia, with the help of Garibaldi's campaign in Southern Italy, he brought about the first Kingdom of Italy in 1861 which, with the exception of Rome and Venice, effectively unified the country. However, whether he united Italy as a nationalist or took it over on behalf of the House of Savoy (Northern Italy) by a quasi-colonial strategy remains a subject of debate up to the present. At all events, between them these three figures represented the three necessities of anticolonial strategy: the brilliant general, the intellectual who supplied the nationalist ideology, and the astute diplomat who could negotiate successfully with national and imperial governments. The Italian case was more complicated than that of a typical colony, given that Italy was landed with a whole range of occupying European and Italian powers who all had interests in the country, to say nothing of the complication of the Vatican, whereas in general for most colonies there was only one external power to deal with. Italy nevertheless provided an example for international revolutionary movements of the necessary political, military, and cultural strategies for achieving independence, as well as, finally, an inspirational and highly publicized example of success.

Anticolonialists also looked to the example of Ireland, which had struggled against English rule since the eighteenth century. Irish rebellion had begun with the United Irishmen in 1798, but moved into the form of parliamentary battles for Catholic emancipation led by Daniel O'Connell after union with Britain in 1800. In the 1830s, with O'Connell's campaign seeming to be getting nowhere, a Young Ireland movement was developed as a nationalist political party. In 1848, in the time of the Famine and also the year of popular European revolutions, Young Irelanders led by William Smith O'Brien staged an unsuccessful rebellion and were subsequently transported to Tasmania. By the 1850s, some of those who had participated in the rebellion founded the Irish Republican Brotherhood with a view to achieving independence through armed rebellion (the resort to arms would later be followed by the Irish Republican Army, and subsequently by the groups variously known as the IRA, Official IRA, Provisional IRA, and Real IRA). Supported by the Fenian Brotherhood in the United States, the IRB staged spectacular acts of terrorism in mainland Britain and elsewhere. Fully utilizing the resources of the invention by Alfred Nobel, the Swedish arms manufacturer and later financial source of the Nobel prizes, of easily portable nitroglycerin – dynamite – in 1867, the IRB developed the world's first international terrorist movement, bombing not only English cities, but also striking around the world with attempted assassinations of royalty in Australia and New Zealand, an invasion of Canada, and numerous small uprisings (Young 2011). One of the effects of the Fenian invasion of Canada in 1866 was to encourage the British government to turn "British North America" into a single state, leading to the Canada Act of 1867. The second half of the nineteenth century also saw the appearance of a range of other nationalist political movements, from Michael Davitt's Land League which initiated the Land War, to Douglas Hyde's Gaelic League, as well as active military involvement such as John MacBride's Irish Brigade, which fought on the side of the Boers during the Boer War from 1899 to 1900. But it was the supreme act of self-sacrifice offered by James Connolly, Patrick Pearse, and the other participants of the Easter Rebellion of 1916, announced with a formal declaration of independence, that became the most spectacular event of Irish resistance, its nobility commemorated in W. B. Yeats' famous poem, "Easter 1916": "All changed, changed utterly: / A terrible beauty is born." Although the Rebellion itself was put down by the British without mercy and seemed to have failed, it did not escape anyone's notice that by 1922 ungovernable Ireland had finally become a free state. More ominously, it did so by becoming one of the first partitioned states of the twentieth century. What was unique about Ireland compared to anywhere else from a nationalist or anticolonial point of view was the consistency of its struggle for well over a hundred years and its untiring determination, as well as the inventive range of different strategies that were pursued: it offered a continuous, undefeated example of resistance.

The Bolshevik Revolution, 1917

Italy and Ireland offered the great examples of nationalist quasi-anticolonial rebellion. But scarcely a year after the Easter Rising another event occurred that would change anticolonial thinking until the end of the century: the Bolshevik Revolution.

It was Marx and his followers, particularly the Bolsheviks under Lenin, who formulated the most cogent arguments against imperialism as a system of exploitation driven not by the high ideals of civilization but capitalism's need for profit. From a colonized person's point of view, what was revolutionary about the Russian Revolution was not so much its communism *per se* as the fact that the Soviet Union was established as the first state committed to an anti-imperial politics and the liberation of the colonies: up to that point, all of the world powers had been imperial rivals, none of them had challenged the imperial system as such. The Bolshevik Revolution was therefore a pivotal moment for anti-imperialism, as it moved for the first time into the register of state power. Communism represented a challenge and threat to empire; until 1989 anticolonial combatants of all kinds were frequently characterized simply as "communists." After 1917, anti-imperial activities around the world were supported by the Soviet Union's Third International, which held influential congresses on colonialism and gave material support. The formation of communist parties throughout the world created an international network of disciplined local organizations that would be put into effective service in the independence campaigns that followed 1945 (Young 2001: 115–157). Though most communists continued to believe that working-class revolution would come in the advanced industrial states rather than the colonies, the Third International was active in coordinating revolutionary organizations such as the League Against Imperialism in the 1920s (Petersson 2013). In the 1930s under Stalin, communist internationalism waned, but resurfaced powerfully during the fight against fascism in World War II, for example in Greece, and the battle against colonialism subsequently. After the communist victory in China in 1949, a second major communist power began actively to support anticolonial movements, particularly in Southeast Asia, above all Vietnam.

Although its discourse became increasingly mixed with Marxist rhetoric and ideas, for the most part anticolonialism remained deeply nationalist in inspiration and drew on nationalist sentiment in order to develop popular support. Anticolonialist combatants were attracted by the promises of socialism as well as its rhetoric of anti-imperialism, but the difficulty was that communism, being internationalist, was politically also anti-nationalist. However, in practice the USSR allowed communists to make strategic alliance with nationalists, as in China. After 1945, contrary to the doctrine of European – and Indian – Marxism, third-world socialist anticolonialism increasingly combined nationalism with socialism, as is evident in the writings of Amilcar Cabral (1973) or Frantz Fanon (1966). In order to align the two more effectively, and to mediate communist doctrine to their own realities, third-world anticolonialists followed the example of Mao Zedong by discarding the revolutionary figure of the worker for the peasant.

Anticolonialists were therefore also internationalists: they looked to other anticolonial groups for inspiration, solidarity, or even aid. This was augmented by the paradoxical situation that many anticolonial activists lived in the European capitals, in part because the political liberties that existed there were suppressed in the colonies. It also allowed them to interact with other anticolonial militants, either individually or through Comintern conferences, or other gatherings such as the "Nationalities and Subject Races Conference" held in London in 1910, or communist organizations such as the League Against Imperialism. Internationalism also produced contact with radical groups in Europe and North America, above all between African and Caribbean anticolonial activists and African American radicals such as the Trinidadian George Padmore and the African American W. E. B. Du Bois (the Jamaican black nationalist Marcus Garvey, though forging links between the United States, the Caribbean and Africa, kept his Universal Negro Improvement Association [UNIA] relatively separate from those of other activists). These links were consolidated through the Pan-African Congresses which met from 1900 to 1994 (the most famous was the fifth, held in Manchester in 1945, organized by Kwame Nkrumah and George Padmore). Utilizing imperial rivalries as a form of support was also an important tactic. Indian Ghadarite nationalists conspired with Germany during World War I, while there was also cultivation of fascist regimes during the 1930s. The most famous opportunist in this context was Subhas Chandra Bose who founded the Nazi Indische

Legion in Germany in 1941 and then in 1943 revived the Indian National Army (INA) that had been created by the Japanese after the fall of Singapore in 1941. The INA then took part in the Japanese Burma campaign, assisting in the unsuccessful attempt to invade India in 1944. The Japanese and Indian National armies were defeated, at great human cost, by the British Fourteenth Army, a Commonwealth army which consisted predominantly of units from the Indian army, along with some British and African colonial troops (Bayly and Harper 2005).

Anticolonial politicians in different colonies learnt from each other: where one strategy was judged to have been particularly successful, it then influenced the behavior of others elsewhere around the globe. After the British left India in 1947, it seemed that the Gandhian principle of non-violence was the most effective means of achieving independence, so non-violence became the chosen path of other leaders challenging the British, such as Nkrumah in Ghana. On the other hand, in 1954 when the French were decisively defeated by the Vietnamese at Dien Bien Phu and agreed to withdraw from Indochina altogether, the Front de Libération Nationale (FLN) began their armed insurrection in Algeria. After the first colonies became independent, their leaders continued the tradition of international cooperation, most notably at the Bandung conference of non-aligned nations in 1955 and the Conference of the Organization of the Solidarity of the Peoples of Asia, Africa, and Latin America (known as the Tricontinental) held in Havana in 1966 (Young 2005a).

Strategies of Resistance: Rebellion or Reform

The practical question for anticolonial movements was how to make them effective: the alternatives were revolution or reform, the American way of armed rebellion of 1776 or the other American way that had been formulated in 1849 by Henry David Thoreau in response to his distaste for slavery and imperialism (specifically, the recent Mexican–American War) in the United States: civil disobedience (Thoreau 2008). Thoreau's ideas, including his preference for simple living, inspired Mahatma Gandhi as a strategy for peaceful protest and resistance against British rule. Starting with his campaigns against the South

African government in the 1890s, Gandhi developed a whole ethos of non-violence, *satyagraha* ("soul" or "truth force"), which enabled him to assert a moral high ground in the face of any form of brutal oppression and to claim higher ethical values than the colonizer. Drawing on resistance techniques learnt from Thoreau, Irish nationalists, and suffragettes, Gandhi's campaigns galvanized ordinary Indians while maintaining the respect of the British and gaining admiration and emulation around the world (in the 1960s, Martin Luther King drew directly on his example for the conduct of the Civil Rights movement in the United States).

In practice the path of liberation varied between relatively peaceful negotiation in the case of exploitation colonies (for example in India, Ghana, or Uganda) and violent warfare for settlement colonies, where a significant presence of colonial settlers produced often apparently intractable situations, such as in Algeria or Rhodesia. However, not all exploitation colonies were liberated without violence (Vietnam would be an obvious example), while some settler colonies, such as the former German colony of Tanganyika, were decolonized relatively peacefully. Similarly, even peaceful decolonizations were not without the use of violence: India was relatively speaking non-violent but the name of Bhagat Singh reminds us that it also saw many forms of violent insurrection, from Pulithevar in Tamil Nadu in the 1750s, to the 1857 Rebellion, to the 1930 Chittagong Armoury Raid, to the Indian National Army's attempted invasion in 1944. Indeed Gandhi was prompted to write his manifesto *Hind Swaraj* advocating non-violence after meeting violent Indian revolutionaries in London. In Ireland over the centuries all strategies were tried – armed rebellion, reformism, armed rebellion again, cultural resistance, non-violent resistance, and armed rebellion once again. Although Gandhi's example remained influential in the 1950s, after the success of the Cuban Revolution in 1959 and Algerian independence in 1962, in the 1960s most anticolonial movements, even the hitherto peaceable Gandhian South African National Congress, turned to armed rebellion (Young 2005b).

In a world of imperialists, and therefore in the absence of international support, armed insurrections in the colonies were rarely successful after the liberation of the Americas. Even Bolshevik backing after 1917 was in practice more useful in terms of effecting organization than producing revolution. The organizational weakness of anticolonial rebellion would be decisively changed by the Leninist model of party organization that enabled the colonized to develop successful revolutionary strategies. It was the Bolsheviks who invented the powerful model of the popular or liberation "front," in which all the different oppositional constituencies were brought together so that the controlling power would face a single opponent. This technique was used successfully in Vietnam, Algeria, El Salvador, and elsewhere. The failure to develop a national liberation front in India meant that the country achieved independence only through its division into separate national states that corresponded to the two main anticolonial parties, Congress and the Muslim League. A number of national liberation fronts have since developed in India, this time in an attempt by regional ethnic groups to win self-government, for example in Assam, Manipur, Tripura, and West Bengal.

Organization, though strategically useful, was not however enough in itself. What really changed the possibilities for armed rebellion was the development of the Cold War after 1945. The United States' commitment to national liberation was tempered by the preference of natives to choose socialism over capitalism, just as in the twenty-first century its enthusiasm for spreading democracy around the world was tempered by the experience of electors in democratic elections choosing Hamas and the Muslim Brotherhood in Gaza and Egypt. Communism came to be seen as the greater threat, with the result that most anticolonial activists turned to the Soviet Union and China for support. The Cold War was then fought out in proxy hot wars in the colonies, in Angola, in Cambodia, in the Congo, in Malaya, in Vietnam, and elsewhere, particularly in Central and South America.

Culture as Soft Power

The alternation of peaceful and violent anticolonialism mirrored the strategies of the colonists themselves. Although the colonial power proved its military superiority by the very fact of occupation, this hardly legitimized colonial rule. It therefore needed its own version of carrot and stick, peaceful and violent tactics, in order to maintain its power and authority. The first strategy was to achieve supremacy and profit by controlling the basic infrastructure – along with the military and police, through taxes and law. At the same time, all occupying forces attempted to produce consent among local people – the greater the consent, the easier the control. The colonial power therefore typically suggested that it had intervened not for its own interest or profit but for the benefit of the local people. Though Christianity was usually on offer, this was not necessarily very palatable to the locals. More powerful and more attractive was the very fact of power itself, and by extension the culture of which it formed a part: both were presented with maximum visibility and charisma in order to impress and persuade the colonized. Although it was not usually formulated in such terms at the time, this characteristic of the colonial ruler is generally characterized today with the term "modernity."

European colonizers did not just arrive and claim that their own culture, language, and religion were as superior as their military might, though they did suggest that. They also assumed that their culture was "modern," while the local culture was inherently inferior, stuck in the past. The idea that European culture was inherently better at every level certainly seems to have been the attitude of early travelers to the Americas, armed with their various forms of Christianity. But those who went East, to India and China, originally had the opposite reaction, since the local cultures seemed so superior in many respects to their own, from their commodities to architecture to technology to government organization to sheer wealth. Toward the end of the eighteenth century, however, with the development of Enlightenment ideas of rationality, and the fast development of science in the same period, the idea began to circulate that human beings in Europe had emerged into a superior state of being, with the rest of humanity being imagined as still caught in mental darkness of various kinds, a view memorably projected by Immanuel Kant in his essay "An Answer to the Question 'What is Enlightenment?,'" which begins with the phrase "Enlightenment is man's emergence from his self-imposed immaturity." That emergence implicitly leaves all those without enlightenment in a state of permanent childhood.

In conditions of sustained colonial rule, it does not take long for the power of the occupiers to be transmitted to everything associated with the culture that has come with them – dress, language, literature, history, music, and art. Local ways and customs begin to seem old-fashioned and behind the times. We can see this process of culture as soft power occurring in nineteenth-century India, when a local poet such as Michael Madhusudan Dutt (1824–73) discarded his own Bengali and began writing poetry in English instead. Upper-class Indians who had profited from colonial rule, particularly by practicing law, began to show their status by rejecting native dress and wearing western clothes (even Gandhi as a young man wore a dapper European suit with a stiff collar and tie). Frantz Fanon later characterized this as the first phase of colonial culture, when the local people absorb and appropriate the colonizer's culture in all its dimensions, beginning with its language (Fanon 1966: 165–199). Perhaps the most extreme example of this colonial mimicry took place not in the colonial sphere but as a means of avoiding colonization: after 1868, having been forced by American and European powers to open up for trade, Japan responded with a radical policy of self-modernization, adopting not only the military technology and customs of European armies, but discarding wholesale many traditional forms of its own culture for European customs, from wearing formal evening dress to eating beef.

The group that personally benefitted most from this phase was women, some of whom were able to utilize western practices in order to liberate themselves from restrictive cultural norms prevalent in traditional patriarchal societies and enjoy benefits such as education or legal rights. Colonial rule was disempowering for the colonized society in general, but for women it could also provide opportunity or potential for redress (Chandra 2008). Even indentured labor was utilized as an opening for some runaway or outcast colonized women (Bahadur 2013). European and American women on occasion also found that empires offered chances for self-advancement that would have been impossible at home, even if it involved serving rather than contesting imperial aims (Chaudhuri and Strobel 1992; Jayawardena 1995; Woollacott 2001). During the anticolonial period, colonized women were also particularly active, as organizers, campaigners, and combatants, even if none of them compared to the prominent role played by the Rani of Jhansi, the most charismatic leader of the 1857 Indian rebellion (McClintock 1995; O'Gorman 2011; Sangari and Vaid 1989; Singh 2014; Young 2001: 360–382).

On National Culture

Some colonial subjects, such as the Bengali writer Nirad C. Chaudhuri, never moved away from the phase of admiring imitation of colonial culture; in most colonial societies, however, such sentiments were succeeded by a nationalist reaction, which as Singh notes, was in turn brought into being through the realm of culture. Edward Said puts it in a different way: "Because of the presence of the colonizing outsider, the land is recoverable at first only through the imagination" (Said 1993: 271). Resistance through the imagination was a primary form of response for subordinated people, just as it continues to be in the West Bank and Gaza in the twenty-first century. It can take many forms: in the course of the nineteenth and twentieth centuries, anticolonial artists, intellectuals, and politicians produced a huge volume of material designed to challenge colonial ideology, to retrieve their own repressed culture, theorize their own political practices, and to develop new local cultural forms for the future. These ranged from anthropological works (Jomo Kenyatta), to political theory (Gandhi, Mao, José Carlos Mariátegui), to fiction (Premchand, Raja Rao), to history (C. L. R. James), to memoir (Jawaharlal Nehru), to poetry (Aimé Césaire, Ho Chi Minh, Léopold Senghor), to cultural theory (Amilcar Cabral). Gandhi's works alone extend to almost a hundred volumes. In the overall context of anticolonial production of the kind envisaged by Bhagat Singh, this body of work remains unparalleled in its range and rich complexity (Young 2001: 193–359).

As Fanon describes it, the initial phase of imitation of the colonial culture gives way to a second stage of cultural nationalism when nationalists begin to reject the colonial culture on grounds of increasing resistance to colonial rule. Now they look instead to their own past in order to reestablish their own indigenous identity. At this point, everything connected to the colonizer becomes suspect: imported manufactures are rejected, native languages are reappraised, revalued, and chosen over the colonial idiom, local literature is rediscovered and championed, new works are written, and western clothes discarded in favor of indigenous dress. One man widely associated with this reactive stage is the Senegalese poet and politician Léopold Senghor, the inventor of the concept of *négritude*, which revalued the whole of black

African culture as something of supreme cultural value rather than as outdated primitivism as Europeans had claimed. Logically, this stage of cultural nationalism implied a return to using indigenous languages. Though Senghor continued to write in French, others such as Gandhi rejected English in favor of Gujarati. In the Caribbean where the native language had not survived, Caribbean authors began to write in idiosyncratic styles employing local idioms such as those to be heard in Martinique, a position most fully developed by Fanon's contemporary, the poet Édouard Glissant. Fanon himself advocated a third stage, in which the two were brought together dialectically with culture integrated into the independence conflict, so that, as he put it, the struggle became the national culture. A different way of putting that would be the argument of the famous anticolonial leader and theorist of Guinea-Bissau, Amilcar Cabral, that culture was simply a weapon of resistance (Cabral 1973: 59–60).

Cultural nationalism, while advocating a harmonious and totalizing national culture that embodied the spirit or aspirations of the nation, moved easily into oppositional modes. While Gandhi went so far as to advocate a rejection of modernity as such, criticizing even hospitals and the use of western medicine, in practice most cultural nationalists accepted western technology even if they rejected western culture – just as in the twenty-first century, the most anti-western organizations, such as Boko Harām, do not refuse to use modern weapons – indeed their flag features the AK47. Even Gandhi, despite denouncing the railways and espousing a return to the earlier technology of the spinning wheel, made full use of the modern media for his political campaigns. The acceptance of western science meant that most postcolonial nations at independence remained in full agreement with the ideas of colonial economics, so that the first task was to "develop" the country and take it fully into modernity. Huge, expensive infrastructural projects duly followed.

As Bhagat Singh points out, most anticolonial nationalist movements involve long preparatory movements of cultural revival, which both reestablish the self-confidence of the colonized people and give them a cohesive sense of identity with which to confront the colonizer. As a result, nationalism disdains syncretism in its drive for a cultural renewal that also demands an ahistorical cultural homogeneity. So Singh himself forcefully argues that in the absence of Indians being able to speak one language as a nation, they should at least write all their languages in the same script: tellingly, he complains that Muslims in particular insist on writing in Urdu. The nationalist reaction to colonialism meant that culture was never a secondary factor in anticolonial politics: cultural struggles made up a fundamental part of the overall political struggle. The writings of anticolonial nationalists, from Gandhi to Kenyatta, are replete with claims for the superiority of local culture and the need for renewal, but at the same time this often meant promoting one particular language or form of local culture and not another. Sometimes this could work to significant negative effect, for example the tendency that continues even today to consider it acceptable for men to take on all the trappings of modernity, while trying to protect women in their traditional roles as guardians of time-honored local culture centered on the home (Chatterjee 1993). Many of the issues of cultural difference that historically sparked political confrontation between colonizer and colonized have involved customary practices relating to women: female genital mutilation, child marriage, veiling, widow burning (*sati*). Fanon was one of the few anticolonial male writers and activists who argued that the fight against the colonizer transformed the role of women in their societies in a positive and progressive way (Fanon 1965: 35–67).

At the same time, nationalists wanted to challenge some elements of western culture that were paraded with the authority of science rather than culture. While only Gandhi offered an alternative economic theory to capitalism other than socialism (and his ideas in this area were taken from Carlyle, Ruskin, and the Arts and Crafts movement), all non-western anticolonialists were concerned to deny the ideological science of western racial superiority. One response was to appropriate and invert it: from the *négritude* of Léopold Senghor and Aimé Césaire, to the Japanese version of racial theory, according to which the Japanese were a superior race to other East Asians. Africans, or people of African descent, who had been characterized in the most extreme form in terms of racial inferiority, confronted racialism most directly. They needed to attack the ideology of race in order to dispute European and North American ideas about the form of government that was appropriate for them. Colonial rulers had argued that the people ("natives") that they ruled were not yet fully mature human beings: they were "backward," "primitive," or like children, and therefore not fit to govern themselves (forgetting that they had been governing themselves perfectly well before the Europeans arrived). Anticolonialists therefore had to make two interrelated arguments. It was not enough to quarrel on the basis of human rights, because they were first obliged to claim and prove themselves to be fully human. They had to show that the colonized person was not inferior, not a lower form of human being, but fully human in every sense. We can see Frantz Fanon invoking this idea at the end of *The Wretched of the Earth* where he advocates a new humanism that will include all, not just some, of humanity as human beings. By 1961 that assertion was much easier to make because the ideology of race, and racial discrimination, on which colonialism and imperialism depended, had been discredited as a result of the Holocaust.

9

Decolonization

There were, broadly speaking, three phases of decolonization: *(1) the colonies in the Americas, for the most part during the late eighteenth and early nineteenth centuries; (2) the colonies of Europe that date from the nineteenth century up to the first quarter of the twentieth; and (3) the colonies of the global South in the period from 1945 to the end of the twentieth century. The first involved European settlers (and in Haiti former slaves) in the Americas; the second, European settlers in Canada, South Africa, Australia, and New Zealand, as well as, finally, the Southern Irish, along with Europeans in the Austro-Hungarian and Ottoman Empires; the third, the populations of European colonies in Africa, Asia, the Caribbean, and the Pacific. Although almost all countries in today's world are now post-colonies, their situation differs therefore in relation to the historical era of their emergence as nation-states.

Phase One: 1776–1826

The first period of decolonization was inaugurated by the American Revolution of 1776. For as long as there had been a New France alongside the thirteen British colonies – a vast area of land to the west of the British colonies stretching from Canada to Louisiana – the colonists had had a reason to stay loyal to the British Crown which

Empire, Colony, Postcolony, First Edition. Robert J. C. Young.
© 2015 Robert J. C. Young. Published 2015 by John Wiley & Sons, Ltd.

protected them. The British strategic mistake was to defeat the French and to offer them the choice of retaining either New France or Guadeloupe and Martinique: they chose the latter (the two islands were far more economically profitable). In order to placate the American tribes to the east of the Mississippi who had supported the French, as well as a general sense of responsibility for the well-being of the Native Americans in their colonies, in 1763 the British proclaimed these newly acquired territories a vast Indian reserve and forbade settler expansion westward. Aside from arguments about taxation, the underlying motivation for the settler rebellion that began ten years later was resentment at this prohibition: as soon as independence was achieved, the borders were broken open and the United States reconfigured itself as a land empire expanding ever westward (in 1803, during France's brief period of repossession of the southern parts of French territory, Napoleon took the opportunity of selling Louisiana to the United States). This established the first law of independent colonies: that national sovereignty for the most part leads to a diminution in the well-being of the indigenous people, as far as genocide, or, in non-settler colonies, of ethnic minorities who live in outlying regions or so-called "tribal areas." Marxist critics go one step further, arguing that decolonization often simply involves a transfer of power from the colonizer to the local bourgeoisie or comprador classes. As the narrator of Aravind Adiga's novel *The White Tiger* puts it: "In 1947 the British left, but only a moron would think that we became free then" (Adiga 2008: 22).

Successful colonial rebellion in the North soon produced rebellion throughout the Americas: in Haiti (San Domingue) the first, and last, successful slave revolt, and then in other colonial territories after the Napoleonic invasion of Spain. Threatened by Spanish and Napoleonic forces in 1807, the entire Portuguese royal court was shipped by the British navy to Brazil, which then declared independence from Portugal in 1822. By 1826, most of the states of Central and South America had achieved independence. With the exception of Haiti, all these new independent states were further examples of the kind of colonial anticolonialism that had developed in the United States: rebellion for the most part not by the indigenous or slave population against the colonized, but by the settlers against the colonial government in Europe. In order to keep up their racial hierarchy over indigenous peoples, the settler population attempted to maintain their identity as Europeans, with the result that they were propelled into a mentality of dependency for the next hundred and fifty years. Being colonists who lived far away in a different cultural, political, and economic environment, they could never quite manage to be fully European and could only ever lag behind the cultures of Europe that were changing dramatically as a result of the industrial revolution and its related political developments. Haiti, meanwhile, remained a one-off, its independence unrecognized for decades by the United States or most European states. Catastrophically, in 1825 it was forced into punitive indemnity payments by France to compensate for the lost value of French property including slaves, the debt contributing to the subsequent instability of its government and the ruin of its economy. These conditions persisted into the twentieth century – from 1914, Haiti was reoccupied for twenty years by the United States on the basis of the Monroe Doctrine. The indemnity to France was not paid off until 1947. In 2003 the Haitian President Aristide requested that France return the unjust indemnity payments, now valued at $21 billion; he was removed shortly afterward in a military coup. France, which in 2014 had a GDP of $2.8 trillion compared to Haiti's $7.9 billion, has yet to pay up.

 It was in the initial period of decolonization in the late eighteenth century that modern democracy was first instituted in the world as a result of anticolonial revolution. The United States offered the ideology not only of liberty, which the founding fathers thought of as derived from English traditions, but also of democracy, a radical political system that was regarded by European conservatives somewhat akin to the way that communism was seen in the twentieth century. For many autocratic or oligarchic regimes around the world, from China to Egypt to North Korea, it continues to be a dangerous concept: think Tiananmen Square. Anticolonial revolution thus produced not only the first postcolonial but also the first democratic state in the modern world, a state that, quite remarkably, has endured to the present day in its original revolutionary form, which is certainly an impressive testimony to its founders. Although inspired by the example of the United States, the other newly independent settler colonies in South America came to be ruled as oligarchies of various kinds.

Of course, democracy in the United States as in ancient Greece did not originally include everyone: slaves, African Americans, Native Americans, and women were excluded. Universal suffrage would not come for almost two hundred years, until 1965. What is remarkable, in fact, about full democracy is what a recent system it is. Although France originally introduced universal suffrage for all males over 25 years of age in 1792, it had to be reestablished in 1875, since when it has continued unbroken. In 1848 Switzerland was the first country to institute universal male suffrage that has continued ever since – however, it only adopted universal female suffrage in 1990. The first country to institute universal suffrage nationally was a colony, New Zealand, in 1893. Australia followed suit in 1902, though the same legislation barred indigenous people from voting, so the suffrage there was hardly universal: it only became so in 1967. Despite a fondness for lecturing on democratic values to the rest of the world, therefore, western democracies have in fact only established universal suffrage relatively recently, usually after long and contentious civil campaigns to do so. For their part, it is hardly surprising that some former colonies have found it difficult to maintain themselves as full democracies when the system was only suddenly brought in at the moment of decolonization. They too, as western countries did, often have to go through years of effort to achieve it, maintain it, broaden it. Similarly, those countries that never became full democracies on decolonization, such as many of those in the Middle East, are also obliged to go through the same fights against authoritarianism as western countries went through in the past, though now largely forgotten. Historically, in all countries, democracy has been realized through continuous struggle, and since it is unlikely ever to be fully achieved, it will always require a permanent effort to maintain the democracy of the present and to work toward the fuller democracy of the future.

Phase Two: 1826–1945

In 1821 Russia announced an edict (*ukase*) over Northwestern America as far south as the 51st Parallel, from modern Alaska to British Columbia, and the following year seized a US ship that was sailing in the region.

Partly in response to this, in 1823 the United States announced what became known as the Monroe Doctrine, guaranteeing that the newly independent countries in the Americas would not become prey to other imperial ambitions, and stating that any further attempts by Europeans or Russia to colonize the Americas, or to interfere with the constituent states of the Americas, would be considered by the United States as an act of aggression. The independence of the new postcolonial states was secured, and henceforth the Americas were protected from being reappropriated by the European empires (though this did not stop European fleets from arriving in the harbors of Caribbean or South American states to pressurize them into paying alleged debts, or France, which improbably claimed a racial kinship with "Latin" America, from invading Mexico in 1838–9 and 1862–7). The advantage to the United States was that it left the whole of the continent free for it to trade with, though in practice throughout the nineteenth century the British were at least as busy trading as the United States was. For South American states, however, the downside of the Monroe Doctrine was that in practice, by the early twentieth century, it meant that the United States at times treated Central and South America a little in the manner of a personal fiefdom, sending in the Marines at will to change or maintain governments, or declaring a protectorate over Panama from its independence in 1903 until 1939 (the Panama Canal was not ceded to Panama until December 31, 1999).

By the 1820s, the first great empires of the Spanish, Portuguese, British, and French had been lost. It might be thought that this would give would-be imperialists some pause for thought. As a result of their experience with the American colonists, and in the face of the development of a "colonial nationalism" in some settler colonies (Jebb 1905), the British reconfigured their empire into a federal model, and encouraged the white settler colonies to become independent "dominions": by 1910 Canada, Australia, New Zealand, and South Africa were independent, though still forming part of the British Empire. How far they continued as *de facto* settler colonies is another matter. Of the remaining British settler colonies, only Kenya and Rhodesia continued to be under direct imperial control. For a while the British, particularly under Gladstone's government, also nominally pursued a policy of resistance to further colonial expansion, famously even handing the

Ionian Islands over to Greece in 1864. Many other European countries, however, became actively acquisitive imperialists, particularly France and Belgium, then Germany, and finally Italy. Russia was also continuously expanding its land empire, while by 1894 Japan had successfully turned itself into an imperialist state on the western model. As a result, the nineteenth century was the second period of great colonial expansion – which paradoxically coincided with the second period of decolonization.

Both Napoleon's invasion and occupation of Europe, and the colonial wars around the globe that took place as part of the Napoleonic Wars, produced a major reconfiguration of the world map. After his failed colonization of Egypt, Napoleon concentrated on creating an empire within Europe, known as the Greater French Empire. In occupying Germany and Italy, Napoleon unwittingly initiated the motor for the nation-states that would eventually follow. His eventual defeat by Britain, Russia, and the Austro-Hungarian Empire meant that monarchical power was reimposed for a time upon all of Europe, including France itself. One consequence of that was that, within Europe, nationalism developed into a powerful political force. The result was that the Austro-Hungarian Empire in particular, despite its liberalism, existed in a state of constant friction throughout the nineteenth century. The Russian Revolution and the end of World War I resulted in the dismemberment of the Russian and Austro-Hungarian Empires, producing independent Czechoslovakia, Hungary, Lithuania, Poland (all in 1918), and Finland (1919). Two better-known independence struggles in this period have already been discussed in chapter 8. One was the unification of Italy, or Risorgimento, generally considered to have lasted for over a hundred years between 1815 and 1918, which was another major long-term effect of Napoleon's adventures. The other spectacular decolonizing event of the period to 1945 was the partial independence of Ireland in 1922.

These states, however, were by no means the only colonies to achieve independence in the period. The main target of anticolonial strategies, largely by the European imperial powers themselves, was the Ottoman Empire. As its name suggests, this was another empire, so in theory it should have fitted perfectly into the imperial system that developed in the course of the nineteenth century. A non-European empire, however, was considered antiquated and out of date. It was a Muslim empire that had survived from an earlier age, the center of the Islamic faith, a religion that most westerners in the nineteenth century assumed was dying out. European powers, therefore, encouraged various nationalisms in order to break it up.

The Ottoman Empire was a land empire stretching, the long way round, from just east of Vienna as far as the western border of modern Algeria. Although not as far-reaching as earlier Muslim empires at their greatest extent, the Ottomans dominated Eastern Europe and the East and South Mediterranean for centuries. Just as in the Austro-Hungarian Empire, in the nineteenth century, the growth of nationalism produced widespread unrest, beginning with the Greek War of Independence. Greece had been under Ottoman rule since 1453. Its growing importance to European intellectuals as the (partly mythic) origin of European civilization meant that the Greeks had a special place in the European mind: Byron's gesture of going to fight in their support in 1823 was characteristic. To great European satisfaction, independence was achieved in 1832. From this point, despite the general system of tolerance for other religions within the Ottoman Empire, Europeans increasingly considered it unacceptable that European Christians elsewhere should be ruled by the Muslim Ottomans, and therefore became more and more prone to meddle in Ottoman affairs. In 1878 at the Congress of Berlin, the independence of several Balkan states – Montenegro, Romania, Serbia, and Bulgaria as a client state of Russia – was agreed between the European powers and the Ottoman Empire. A further condition was that the Austro-Hungarian Empire would occupy the Ottoman province of Bosnia-Herzegovina: its later annexation of it in 1908 would precipitate the nationalist reaction that led to World War I.

It was a very different matter for Arabs. The power vacuum left after Napoleon's invasion of Egypt (1798–1801) had been filled in 1805 by Muhammad Ali, an Albanian who had been in Egypt in service of the Ottomans. Under his rule, Egypt achieved effective independence – until Britain took control of the country in 1882 in order to ensure that it had power over the Suez Canal. The European reaction to Arab nationalism was very different to that of the Greeks, and characteristic of the general attitude toward non-Europeans that would prevail right up to World War II: Arab nationalist unrest under the Ottomans was encouraged, but only so that the country itself could be appropriated as another colony by the Europeans themselves. At times, European powers simply picked off parts of the Ottoman Empire that they calculated that the Ottomans would be unable to defend, from the French invasion of Algeria in 1830 to the Italian appropriation of Libya in 1911. By 1923, the whole of the Ottoman Empire had been carved up by Europeans into different segments, and the political map of the modern Middle East created by fiat of the victorious allied powers (Barr 2012). Only one strategy went wrong at the time: the attempt to dismember not only the empire but also most of Turkey itself by partitioning it between Greece, Italy, a new Kurdish state, the French, and the British, at the Treaty of Sèvres (1920) failed spectacularly and proved unenforceable. The so-called "sick man of Europe" proved to be remarkably resilient. In what Turks call their "War of Independence" (that is, independence from proposed colonization), the Turkish army, under its charismatic leader Kemal Atatürk, defeated the invasion armies of the British, Greeks, French, and Italians, as well as crushing the Armenian forces of the short-lived Armenian state that had been established in 1918. By 1920 Armenia had been annexed by the Soviet Union, where it would remain until 1991. It was not only the Turks who turned out to be unexpectedly resilient: in 2013, almost a hundred years after the contours of the map of the Middle East had been drawn up in secret in 1916 by the British and French diplomats Sir Mark Sykes and François Georges-Picot, those divisions were challenged outright for the first time by the jihadist Islamic State of Iraq and Syria: "Smashing Sykes–Picot" they tweeted to their followers as they bulldozed a berm between Iraq and Syria in June 2014. In the same year, the group proclaimed a Caliphate (a traditional form of Islamic state) and named their leader, Abu Bakr al-Baghdadi, Caliph. The last Caliphate had been abolished by Atatürk in 1924. Islamists have a long memory.

Just as Ireland finally won independence as the cost of being partitioned in 1922, so too in the various conferences and treaties that followed World War I the principle of nationalism and its equation with particular ethnic groups meant that politicians resorted to the practice of dividing and engineering the populations of whole countries, extending the principle of eugenics to that of nations. A nation-state was supposed to correspond to the ethnic group of the people who lived there. Unfortunately in most places, then as now, people were mixed in altogether different ways, either through historical movements as in Central Asia, or through earlier political configurations, such as the Holy Roman Empire, as a result of which Germans were dispersed all over Eastern Europe, or the Ottoman Empire, under which groups of Ottomans were encouraged to settle in the Balkans so as to disperse local power and appropriate the territory more fundamentally than as an occupied colony (settlers in modern Tibet or the West Bank serve a comparable function). In 1923 the diverse milieu of the Ottoman Empire was reverse engineered, with millions of Greeks and Turks sent "back" to what had been declared their own countries from those in which they lived. So Greeks were moved out of cosmopolitan Smyrna (Izmir) and the surrounding region in what became Turkey, and millions of Turks were sent packing from the equally cosmopolitan Thessaloniki already conquered by the Greeks in 1912. The first of several attempts at creating nations out of the heterogeneous peoples of the Balkans resulted in the creation of "Yugoslavia." The same partitioning process and population transfer would be attempted after World War II in the Middle East in Palestine, and in South Asia with the creation of India and Pakistan (Hobsbawm 1990: 132–133). Though much less is heard about it today, during and after the two world wars a comparable population movement was also engineered across central-Eastern Europe. The city of Łódź in Poland can serve as an example of this history: successively cleansed over the course of the twentieth century of its population of Germans, Jews, Roma, and Russians.

The destruction of World War I produced in its aftermath a burst of nation creation, and advocacy of the principle of national self-determination, affirmed by the American President Woodrow Wilson in 1918 in a stark change of policy from his imperialist predecessor Theodore Roosevelt. The new mood came as a response to the perceived socialist threat of the 1917 Bolshevik Revolution, and the Soviet government's espousal of national self-determination and support for struggles against imperialism. Although Wilson raised many hopes (W. E. B. Dubois organized the first Pan-African Congress in Paris in 1919 to petition the politicians meeting at the Versailles Peace Conference for African independence), in practice he was outwitted by the British and French, who used the defeat of Germany and the

Ottomans to appropriate their respective colonial territories in Africa, the Middle East, and the Pacific (where the spoils were also shared by Australia and Japan) and expand their own empires. However, it was not only in Turkey that things did not entirely go as planned: as a result of a popular uprising in Egypt in 1919, the British were obliged to grant Egypt independence in 1922, though they continued to maintain troops there until 1954. The new territories in the Middle East also proved harder to subdue than anticipated, and the air force was brought in to bomb the people into submission: but by the 1930s, as a result of local resistance, they were being granted independence – Iraq in 1932, Syria in 1936, and the Lebanon in the same year, though the French government never succeeded in getting the latter ratified by its own parliament before France had itself fallen to the Germans. Independence was only declared in 1943 after the Vichy regime in Lebanon had been expelled by the British and Free French.

Outside the Middle East, the 1930s was rather the era of further colonizations, as Nazi Germany tried to turn itself into the Greater Germanic Reich by annexing Europe and large parts of Russia. Even the Soviet Union's policy of internationalist revolution was terminated in favor of socialism in one country (which itself included some new as well as traditional Russian colonies). In the East, for their part the Japanese continued their imperial expansion in this period. They had already annexed parts of China and Korea, and, as allies of Britain and France in World War I, had seized the German concessions in China and colonies in the Pacific. In 1937 the Japanese conquered Manchuria. Having signed a pact with Germany and Italy, in 1940 the Japanese began to invade colonies in Southeast Asia: Australian Papua (New Guinea), British Burma, Hong Kong, and Malaya, French Indo-China, American Philippines, and Dutch Indonesia. In seizing these colonies, they drew on the anticolonial concept of the "Greater East Asia Co-Prosperity Sphere," proposed by the Marxist philosopher Kiyoshi Miki, to represent themselves as anticolonial liberators; before surrendering in 1945, they granted some of them, such as Indonesia, independence. Such gestures augmented the expectations of many in the erstwhile colonies that they would become independent at the end of the war. However, many of the former colonizers had different ideas and expected simply to take back control for themselves.

Phase Three: 1945–Present

The third phase of decolonization, which followed the defeat of Germany and Japan in 1945, is the best known and documented (Betts 2004; Chamberlain 1999; Springhall 2001). Once again the world maps were redrawn according to the wishes of the victors. Germany had already had its colonies removed in 1918; in the peace treaty of 1947, Italy lost all claim to its colonies, such as Albania, Eritrea, Ethiopia, Libya, and Somaliland, all of which gained independence by 1951, with the exception of Somaliland which became a UN Trust Territory until 1960. In 1946 the United States granted the Philippines independence, a move that had been on the agenda in the 1930s before the Japanese invasion. Under the pressure of war, particularly the defeated Japanese invasion of India, the British had finally promised to quit India. The country, partitioned into India and West and East Pakistan, became independent in August 1947, with Ceylon following suit in 1948. This was not, however, at the time seen as the beginning of the end of empire. Despite expecting their colonies to support them in the fight against German, Italian, and Japanese aggression or occupation, it was not obvious to the victorious or liberated powers that the war would produce the end of their imperial domains. The Dutch attempted to reoccupy Indonesia, despite it having declared its independence two days after the defeat of Japan. Vietnam also declared its independence in 1945 but was reoccupied by the French with the aid of the British and Americans. Between 1945 and 1947, British and American armies even used "Japanese Surrendered Personnel" to regain control of their own, as well as the Dutch and French, colonial empires, particularly in Indonesia and the Philippines. However, as also in Malaya, such military resistance as had been developed against the Japanese was then simply turned against the recolonizer. The wars of independence had begun.

Subsequent decolonization was unplanned, and followed an erratic path, with some countries being given independence as a result of colonial crisis elsewhere (Morocco and Tunisia in 1956, Senegal and French Sudan in 1960), while with others independence was resisted tooth and nail (Algeria, 1962). Broadly speaking, the colonies that European powers found hardest to withdraw from were settler colonies (Algeria, Rhodesia, arguably Angola), while exploitation colonies were decolonized far more easily. Some were abandoned or given independence in defeat (Indochina, 1954) or ungovernability (Palestine, 1948; Aden, 1967), others soon after pyrrhic victories over colonial resistance (Cyprus, 1960; Kenya, 1963), others as a result of war, agitation, or strikes (India, 1947; Ghana, 1957; Belgian Congo, 1960), others simply because colonies nearby were being made independent too (Ceylon, 1948), and others where the colonial power withdrew or handed over power at the end of a treaty or lease (Trucial States, 1971; Hong Kong, 1997). The major remaining colonial powers in 1945 – Britain, France, and Portugal – had no overall program other than the general policy of maintenance of colonial rule until compelled to grant independence. Each colony was taken on a case-by-case basis. Colonies such as Algeria or Rhodesia proved difficult because of settler resistance to the independence movements of local populations: Algerian *colons* attempted a *coup d'état* in France itself in 1958, while the white government of Rhodesia under Ian Smith declared unilateral independence in 1965. The other problematic kind of colony was the small colony, particularly the small island, which appeared too small to become an independent territory. A number of federal solutions were attempted on earlier models used for Canada or Australia; for example, the West Indies Federation made up of British Caribbean colonies; formed in 1958, it was dissolved back into its constituent islands after 1962, after which the majority of them became independent.

Portugal, which remained under a fascist dictatorship until 1974, attempted to resist decolonization for the longest time by forming a multinational empire under a general ideology of "Tropicalismo," a theory of Portuguese Christian multiculturalism formulated by the Brazilian sociologist Gilberto Freyre (Young 2006). In 1961 Portugal lost Goa and its remaining colonies in India after the Indian government invaded and incorporated them into the state of India, as well as its West African fort in Ouidah which was occupied by newly independent Dahomey. Armed resistance, aided by forces from the Soviet Union, broke out in the same year in Portuguese Angola, and developed in the remaining colonies of Guinea and Mozambique within a few years. The colonial wars in Africa that were fought over the next decade weakened Portugal to the extent that it finally produced revolution at home, the eviction of Salazar's successor, and the establishment of democracy in 1974. The new government granted independence to all Portugal's

African territories; East Timor declared independence the following year, while Macau was returned to China in 1999. In the case of East Timor, however, independence was short lived, as it was then invaded by Indonesia, which despite local resistance did not give up control until 1999. The "right" of independent nations to appropriate former colonies for themselves has been one of the running issues of the decolonization period: in 1975 Spain agreed to Moroccan pressure to give up the Spanish Sahara, but subsequent Moroccan occupation was greeted with resistance from the Polisario Front, an indigenous Berber (Sahrawi) organization which claims the country as an independent Sahrawi Arab Democratic Republic.

There were many other related histories that developed in connection with the independence movements: wars fought in countries where colonial defeat was followed by further wars as western powers attempted to retain control of sovereign states (Vietnam); wars fought where minority settler communities remained in control of independent countries (Rhodesia/Zimbabwe, South Africa); wars fought where democracy was repressed by dictators supported by foreign countries resisting the threat of communism (Cuba before 1959, and many countries in Central and South America): the period of decolonization was a period of turmoil, on almost every continent. It was complicated throughout by the Cold War being fought between the Soviet Union and China and the West. Every resistance to colonial rule became absorbed into this larger trajectory: anticolonial activists were not branded as terrorists (as they had been before World War II) but as communists, a strategy which enabled Portuguese or white South Africans to maintain power much more easily. Apartheid in South Africa began to dissolve the very same year that communism collapsed in the Soviet Union: the game was up. With the end of the Soviet Union, Eastern Europe which had been semi-colonized since 1945 was able to break free and assert its full independence, while in 1991 fourteen of the former Soviet republics were able to exercise a right that had been theoretically available to them all the time – to secede from the union. The last of the major empires had unexpectedly disintegrated at a stroke. Expiring communism immediately encountered rising Islamism: the Russia that emerged from the ruins fought two wars to try to prevent Chechnya's secession from spreading to the other Russian federal republics in Northern Caucasia. The second of these wars was officially concluded in 2009, but Islamic insurgency continues in the region, particularly in Dagestan.

A general account such as this of decolonization in the second half of the twentieth century will always fail to give any sense of the vast human, intellectual, and material resources that were marshaled by the independence movements, and the scale of human suffering caused by the necessity for colonized people to agitate and fight for their freedom. The liberation movements are rarely considered from a global perspective, but nevertheless represent an extraordinary historical phenomenon in which millions of people participated in the common struggle against imperialism. This is the real difference with regard to the collapse of the European empires. Few empires in earlier periods had ended as a result of the assertion of a popular will against the occupying power – more common was the situation in which another power would arrive and take control. The concept of the sovereign nation-state, and the existence of international law to guarantee that (in principle at least), meant that for the first time a country could become independent without serious fear of being promptly occupied or taken over by another empire or state. In the twenty-first century, as a result, although there continues to be a small number of colonies, there are few colonies that carry on against the wishes of a majority of the population. More common is the situation that has already been discussed, where a minority wishes to claim independence from within a sovereign state.

The ironies of historical and modern internal colonial situations were brought out in 2013, when the separatist Spanish Catalan party, Esquerra Republicana, sided with Gibraltar (whose population has twice voted against becoming a part of Spain) against its own government when Spain threatened to take the issue of Gibraltar to the UN on an anticolonial ticket. From an international perspective, Spain's leverage with respect to the British colony of Gibraltar, taken in 1704, is somewhat weakened by the existence of its own colonies across the water in Morocco, Ceuta, and Melilla, captured in the fifteenth century, though it somewhat comically insists that there is no comparison between them.

10

Neo-colonialism, Globalization, Planetarity

Neo-colonialism

"Globalization" is a recent word but it is not a recent phenomenon: globalization was already in play by the fifteenth to sixteenth centuries with world trade routes that extended across every ocean and continent (Osterhammel and Petersson 2009). When British soldiers arrived in Kumasi, in modern-day Ghana, in 1895 in the course of the fourth Anglo-Ashanti war, they were astonished to find in the Manhyia Palace, the seat of the Asantehene of Asanteman, a medieval English jug on display, dating from the time of Richard II. In an early example of the restitution of cultural objects, it was taken back to England, and can now be seen in the British Museum.[1] No one knows how it got to West Africa. In one respect at least, international trade in the medieval and early modern periods was much easier than now: instead of 180-odd different national currencies that have to be loss-exchanged through banks for each transaction, there were just two kinds of money, gold and silver, which were accepted almost universally. Currencies were interchangeable: the Lindisfarne hoard discovered in 2003 in Northeast England contained gold and silver coins of the fifteenth and sixteenth centuries not only from England but also from France, the Netherlands, Saxony, and the papal states. Since that time, each century has had its own form of globalization: in the eighteenth century, European wars

Empire, Colony, Postcolony, First Edition. Robert J. C. Young.
© 2015 Robert J. C. Young. Published 2015 by John Wiley & Sons, Ltd.

were fought over colonies all around the world; by the end of the nineteenth century, imperialism formed a global system through physical occupation of most inhabited territory on earth, together with often coercive practices of trade. By 1900, for the first time in human history, communication systems linked all the peoples of the planet, by means of ships and railways that ran to predicted schedules, and by telegraph and telephone cables. In the twentieth century, decolonization into a world of separate states appeared to break up this globalized imperial world back into its constituent parts. However, as Kwame Nkrumah complained in 1965, he and his fellow politicians achieved liberation and sovereignty for Ghana in 1957 only to discover that they remained subject to larger economic forces, markets, and multinational companies that controlled the prices of local crops, the rate of investment, and the ability to borrow (Nkrumah 1965). Not coincidentally, these powers were managed by the very same countries that had formerly been colonial rulers. Nkrumah called this condition of financial control by the big foreign powers "neo-colonialism," but he was really describing a contemporary version of what has also been called "American" or "informal" imperialism without colonies, where control is exerted on independent countries through economic and financial means (see chapter 5).

The situation in 1965 was not quite as oppressive as Nkrumah suggested, since in his time there were two rival economic systems in existence, capitalism and socialism, fronted by the United States and the USSR. During the Cold War, when these countries constituted two major power bases with their own accompanying forms of economic organizations and military muscle, each seeking dominance, politicians in colonies and postcolonial countries were able to play them off against each other to their own advantage, often claiming to be aligned with neither. After 1945, many newly independent countries, having freed themselves from European colonial rule, chose to align their economies informally with the socialist bloc (even if at the same time they claimed non-aligned status), instituting a Soviet-style centrally controlled economy, tightly protected by trade barriers with industries geared to import substitutions, and with strict limits on foreign exchange. Trade with other economies was arranged and controlled by the government rather than private enterprise. With the end of the Cold War and the demise of the Soviet Union around 1989, this state-organized command-economy system collapsed, and with it the whole possibility of an economic alternative to capitalism. Globalization names the situation that followed, in which capitalism has no earthly limits (Glyn 2006).

Globalization: Free Trade and Advanced Technology

The precursor of the presiding ideology and practice of modern globalization was the doctrine of free trade, which at one time stood in opposition to contemporary imperialism. As Lenin observed, "In the most flourishing period of free competition in Great Britain, i.e., between 1840 and 1860, the leading British bourgeois politicians were opposed to colonial policy and were of the opinion that the liberation of the colonies, their complete separation from Britain, was inevitable and desirable" (Lenin 1965: 93). This had been Adam Smith's argument in the eighteenth century against mercantilism, an earlier version of a command economy centrally controlled by the state. By 1846, when the Corn Laws were repealed, his arguments had become so widely accepted that, as Lenin remarks, many in Britain argued that empire itself should give way to a global free-trade market. By the end of the century, however, imperial rivalry, and the prospect of colonies as captive markets for industrial goods produced from Europe, meant that a global system of imperial preference took over and the champions of free trade fell silent or were ignored as irrelevant. Imperial rivalry then descended into world war, followed by the Great Depression and the period of fascism, and then the Cold War. After lying dormant for a hundred years, free trade reemerged as the dominant economic mantra once more in the 1970s in the guise of neoliberal policy in the Reagan and Thatcher eras. Free trade without domestic subsidy or protection became once again the fundamental objective in international trading negotiations. In 1978, after the turmoil of the Cultural Revolution, reformists in China under Deng Xiaoping began to reorganize the economy on a free-market capitalist basis; in 1989 the Soviet Union collapsed and with it its socialist command economy. Finally, in 1991 the last unre-constructed economy of the major Asian powers succumbed to the power of neoliberalism and gave up its distinctive cultural and economic identity, to disappear under a wash of Coca-Cola and Pizza Huts. India was required to open up and restructure its markets in order to secure a bailout from the International Monetary Fund. The triumph of modern capitalism was complete. A single economic orthodoxy became the default economic model for all global financial institutions. Nations rushed to facilitate neoliberal policies by removing exchange controls and other barriers to international investment, willingly renouncing much of their former autonomy as sovereign states. Globalization had arrived in the modern era, with the whole world transitioning to a single economic system, from which there was no escape.

The new political and economic conditions that emerged at the end of the Cold War coincided with a technological transformation that has changed the lives of most people on the planet: the Internet. Through computers or mobile phones, the majority of people on earth became individually interconnected with each other, as well as to every government and institution to which they were subject – today more people have phones than toilets.[2] Data could be accumulated in limitless amounts in order to assist international marketing or uncontrolled political surveillance. Time and space were apparently abolished as communications became instantaneous. Money could be freely moved around the world (by some) at the click of a mouse. Aircraft became capable of flying vast distances without stopping; satellites were positioned around the earth so that everything and everyone could be tracked, with almost nothing too small or remote enough to be invisible. The nature of war began to change, as it shifted from conflicts between states fought by regular armies to new local wars of organized violence (Kaldor 1999; Badie and Vidal 2014). The United States began to employ unmanned drones to carry out extrajudicial killings of individuals or groups regarded as hostile anywhere on earth, without a formal declaration of war or even acknowledgment of responsibility. The remote, anonymous killings and "collateral damage" of the drone became the hallmark of US high-tech power over low-tech non-western peoples. The objective was no longer territorial acquisition but speed, containment, and subjection. However, drone technology is comparatively not that high-tech, and is relatively cheap: drones are likely to become a ubiquitous feature of a globalized world, with, potentially, any number of countries and combatant groups employing them (Chamayou 2013; Luce 2014).

Economics

Though it has been described in many ways, and certainly has a whole range of different characteristics, globalization is first and foremost an economic transformation (Stiglitz 2002). The end of the Cold War meant that, for the first time, the whole of the earth was available for the further development of finance capitalism. The opening up of global markets described by Marx and Engels in *The Communist Manifesto* in 1848 had become limitless. The entire historical period in between, with all of its political ambitions – imperialism, socialism, fascism – had been transformed into nothing more than an extended interruption to capitalism's unstoppable economic trajectory.

What are the principles of the neoliberal economic system on which globalization has been based? David Harvey defines them succinctly: "Neoliberalism is … a theory of political economic practices that proposes that human well-being can best be advanced by liberating individual entrepreneurial freedoms and skills within an institutional framework characterized by strong private property rights, free markets, and free trade" (Harvey 2005: 2). The key objective of neoliberalism is economic growth – that is, each year we should be better off than last year. Growth, by definition, involves constant change and transformation in society: as Marx and Engels pointed out, bourgeois capitalism was a revolutionary doctrine, sweeping away every obstacle in its path. Money and wealth, it seems, are simply created out of nothing, as if by magic. The secret of capitalism's apparently supernatural power is technology, a technology that needs constantly to be developed and improved in order to increase productivity and sustain growth. Along with consumer products, technology can take the form of advances in medicine to save human lives, or military hardware to destroy them. To create the best environment for this life-and-death theatre of innovation, neoliberal economics advocates open markets and the rolling back of government spending, particularly on "non-productive" areas such as social welfare or any enterprises run by the state, even education. Privatization of state industry, reduction of social welfare systems, and an opening up of the local economy to foreign investment, industry, international corporations, and retail chains, duly follow. The result has been in many cases spectacular creation of wealth. Overall, it has lifted large sections of the world's population out of poverty, but also created a new degree of imbalance between the extremely wealthy and ordinary people. More and more countries, western and non-western alike, are becoming "plutonomies," that is countries with a wide discrepancy between the rich and the poor. While neoliberal policies offer incentives for enterprise and start-ups, a widespread effect of such economics for ordinary people has also been the reduction of employment security. A steady job followed for a whole career has been replaced by short-term positions which at their most extreme take the form of a "zero hours" contract in which the employee is employed without being guaranteed any work at all, but remains permanently on call and barred from taking another job. More and more people are technically in casual employment, whether at the professional, managerial, or shop-floor level – it might be the doctor who treats you in an emergency room, the school teacher instructing your children, or the person who serves you at your local supermarket. Along with such shifts, come the privatization of pensions, and the corporatization of public institutions such as hospitals or universities which are required to operate competitively with each other on "market" principles. Patients and students have become "clients" or "customers."

Following the same neoliberal principles, nations have abolished exchange controls, freely allowed local companies to be taken over by corporations from around the world, and created low tax incentives to encourage foreign firms to become domiciled for tax purposes in their own country, with the result that some of the largest international corporations pay negligible or even zero taxes to the countries around the world in which they operate. Investment from abroad is encouraged, which may mean factories and jobs, but it also means that foreign money may pour in and inflate the economy, the exchange rate, the housing market, and a whole range of assets. The advent of foreign investment may then encourage the state (as has happened with India or Turkey) to run deficits that are entirely financed by such inflows. This leaves them vulnerable to the mechanics of pump and dump: a moment of political conflict or unrest, a change of tax rules somewhere else, or a downturn in the market, and such foreign investment just as easily flows out again, leading the currency to crash, rates to rise, and the economy to stall. Such are the processes produced by neoliberal economics in which the nation-state is no longer sovereign with respect to its own economy, but rather locked into a global network of which it is merely a minor component. The winners are, inevitably, less individual states than the transnational and international financiers and corporations who drive the whole process. Arguably, the world is now subject to a new form of empire that mimics the first phase of European global expansion: of autonomous banks, corporations, and hedge and sovereign investment funds (Hardt and Negri 2000). Nkrumah's neo-colonialism was simply the beginning of the new phase of postcolonial finance capitalism.

International corporations have become extraordinary centers of power. While the state seeks to absolve itself from responsibility for its citizens, severely reducing security and welfare, by contrast governments have not shown an equal willingness to let companies, particularly banks, find their own feet and go to the wall if they fail. The political dominance of finance capitalism was made particularly evident in the financial crisis of 2007–8, when many western banks faced collapse as a result of taking on extraordinary risks in the relentless pursuit of profit (Tett 2010). They were bailed out by their respective governments to amounts that at their peak went into the trillions, while very few of the perpetrators were held accountable.[3] This revelation of the bottom line of the neoliberal value system, of banks over people, and the suddenly all-too-visible limits of the ideology of the free market, created profound skepticism in many societies that is also transforming their politics.

Politics and Human Rights

With the rich irony of capitalism, neoliberal economics also sustain the liberal social values which gave them birth and of which they are the expression. So at the same time that dynamic transformational economic processes are being engineered all over the world, those in charge of the world's powerful governments, or the ranks of bureaucrats and intellectuals working in international agencies, charities, and universities, perennially survey the world's nations for signs of infringement of liberal political values (Human Rights Watch is the best known of these).[4] These comprise democracy, free speech, private property, a secular state, and human rights.

How anchored are these social values to the capitalist system in which they were produced? The East Asian example of successful capitalist autocracies suggests that the only requirements in practice are private property and a secular state. Without private property there would be no individual self-interest to drive the system, while a theocratic state might well not see economic development as its primary aim or concern. Capitalism has certainly worked very effectively without democracy, free speech, and human rights – contemporary China is a perfect example. Whether capitalism can be sustained over longer periods without them, however, is a more open question. The tendency in other East Asian "tiger" economies has been for economic growth to be accompanied by increasing political liberalization, as in the other China, Taiwan (officially the Republic of China) or South Korea. Technological innovations such as the Internet are also increasing this liberal pressure, since availability of knowledge also constitutes a fundamental form of freedom. There is often a rough correspondence between the level of democracy and economic prosperity. This does not prove that one produces the other, only that it is certainly hard for democracy to survive without the stable domestic institutions, such as an army under civilian control, a functioning legal system, an effective health system, schools and universities, good transport infrastructure, that are often the product of a history of prosperity and widespread political participation. The question is whether the reverse is true: in the long term, can countries remain stable and prosperous without democracy? Democracy, in turn, assumes a degree of secularity (Asad 2003). The question that follows from that then becomes: is democracy possible without a secular state?

The political values of democracy, secularism, free speech, and human rights are all linked, as we have seen, to the original formation of the nation-state in the eighteenth century: along with private property, these are the things the state is supposed to protect. Such values are strong political concepts in the sense that they have been taken up, endorsed, and championed by people all over the world. They now form part of humankind's cultural memory and expectation. However, this does not mean that they are immune from debate or challenge. Human rights in particular are the most malleable: the concept of rights can be extended at will in all sorts of directions, to include, for example, the right to bear arms, as in the United States. What was considered an incontrovertible human right in the eighteenth century no longer has the same kind of valence in the twenty-first century, whereas others, for example women's rights, or children's rights or gay rights or animal rights, are now widely accepted (though also still resisted). Rights are inevitably the product of particular historical societies and are therefore themselves always subject to change and renegotiation. Some human rights, moreover, such as the right to free speech or sexual orientation, are far more emphasized in political discourse than others, such as parents' right to choose the kind of education that they give to their children (Universal Declaration of Human Rights 26: 3). The danger is that these values become enforced through a kind of complacent western imperialist attitude in which it is assumed that certain rights are the only ones, that "our" way of doing things is the only way, that they should be the primary political and social values in conditions where many other demands, such as freedom from hunger or the need for clean drinking water, are more urgent and relevant. If you are starving to death, what is the use of your right to free speech?

Western countries often forget that though their origins may go back several centuries, their own values have generally only became a foundational feature of western states in the twentieth century, and far from uniformly – fascism, for example, was an equally popular political form in Europe in the first part of the twentieth century. Rights talk in which formerly (and perhaps not so formerly) imperial countries reprimand erstwhile colonies for failing to uphold human rights will always come across as somewhat hypocritical, given the history of the methods of colonial governance. At worst, such talk can become an excuse for military intervention and occupation, a new form of civilizing mission (Moyn 2010). When westerners speak of non-westerners failing to uphold certain western values, or cultural norms, it is rare to find such commentators considering whether those questioning western ways might actually have a point. It often seems inconceivable that westerners could even imagine learning from other political, social, or cultural norms. For a thousand years Europeans viewed the Muslim insistence on cleanliness with amusement until belatedly in the nineteenth century they realized that cleanliness constitutes the single most important factor in maintaining public health.

The open question is whether neoliberal economics are driving western political and cultural values, or whether western political and cultural values are operating in the service of larger economic aims. Capitalism in itself does not give the impression of being anchored to human rights, even if it benefits from the development of the concept of the individual, since the individual is also a consumer. At best, human rights function as part of an international framework for tempering the excesses of autocrats and capitalism alike in the age of globalization. Western or not, they can still mobilize political consciousness all over the world – as in the title of Bob Marley's famous song, written after his visit to Haiti: "Get up, stand up, stand up for your rights!"

Resistance to Globalization

The University

If anticolonial nationalism was the form taken by resistance to imperial globalization, what are its modern equivalents? As in the imperial era, many forms of resistance, such as liberal opposition, offer internal critiques, whereas others involve more direct contestation.

How far does western education also enforce neoliberal economic values? From the perspective of technology or economics, the two are certainly correlated. Research at universities forms a major factor in the production of the technological change that capitalism requires. Even if academics have been largely unsuccessful in resisting the corporatization of the university, many of them remain spokespeople for human values that are incompatible with the worst excesses of neoliberalism. The role of the intellectual, Edward W. Said has argued, should be to maintain a critical attitude toward his or her own society, challenging what is unjust, championing the invisibly oppressed, disturbing assumptions that have become too comfortable: that is one way for intellectuals to make themselves useful, if at times somewhat troubling to those in power (Said 1994). So Wang Hui, a professor of Chinese language and literature at Tsinghua University in China, for example, has spearheaded the New Left movement in China which has highlighted the severe human costs of China's economic reforms.

The function of the humanities in particular has been defined as keeping alive the awareness that the world is populated by humans whose values, and not simply those defined in terms of rights, may differ radically from those of neoliberal economics and all that serves its purposes, such as militarization and securitization – in other words, liberalism against neoliberalism. But how different are they? Ideas in the humanities may help to create the values that neoliberal economics is seeking to establish. Take the concept of "transnationalism," for example, which has enjoyed something of an academic vogue in the twenty-first century. Its valorization of activities and networks that move across nations rather than within them is certainly hostile to the nationalist values of the nation-state, which might seem to be "progressive." At the same time, however, one of the aims of globalization is also to break down the power of the nation-state in order to facilitate ever greater transnational flows of labor, commodities, and finance. Transnationalism holds no contrapuntal argument of resistance to such processes at its core: compare it in this respect with communist internationalism, as originally defined by the Third International. This was also directed against the nation-state, but on the grounds of it being a bourgeois political form that repressed the power of the workers. Their loyalty, it was argued, should be with each other as a class, not with their respective national bourgeois masters. Internationalism in that sense formed an up-front mode of resistance to the status quo, whereas transnationalism, while challenging the power of the nation-state, charts or facilitates the processes of globalization at the same time. For the most part, discussions of cosmopolitanism also espouse a way of being that, whether for the cosmopolitan elite or the cosmopolitan non-elite of the world's millions of migrant workers, constitutes the precise ideology of the global free-labor market that neoliberal capitalism desires (Gilroy 2013; Robbins 2012).

The Anti-Globalization Movements

On the other hand, it can be argued more positively that the revolution in communications that has promoted globalization has also allowed the formation of transnational oppositional groups, whether the anti-capitalist movement, the global justice movement (sometimes called the Movement of Movements), or, indeed, the anti-globalization movement. As these names indicate, such organizations take two forms – either transnational movements in support of particular minorities, or transnational movements that challenge corporatism and financialization in favor of democratic accountability, fair trade, sustainable development, and human rights. While no doubt in many instances they are fundamentally anarchist or socialist in outlook, their political programs are not necessarily against globalization as such but rather challenge the ethos or morality of the particular forms that it has taken. Such groups have been successful in highlighting these issues by mobilizing demonstrations at meetings of international economic organizations, such as the World Trade Organization, or G7 meetings, while holding their own Social Forum meetings around the world. During the financial crisis, they were particularly active, as in the Occupy Wall Street movement. Such resistance movements have been most successful in those western countries that have been driving the processes of globalization, making, for example, international firms accountable for their employment practices around the world. Critics outside the West, however, point to the ways in which western labor activists have discovered a concern for working conditions in third-world countries only at the same moment as those countries have become more competitive than the West.

Resistance to globalization outside the West, meanwhile, takes three forms: first, opposition which correlates with ecological issues, such as the fight against the growing of GM crops. This links directly to the anti-globalization movements. Secondly, a response to the disparities of wealth produced by globalization, and resistance to local poverty and/ or political instability, by migrating to Europe and North America. Migration is usually attempted illegally, or legally on work visas to regions such as the Gulf States whose economies require huge numbers of foreign workers. Whether legal or illegal, such migrants generally find themselves in working conditions that are exploitative in comparison with normal western standards. The third form of resistance is, not surprisingly, least popular among western and indeed many non-western activists: Islamism.

Islamism

The major act of resistance to globalization came with the attacks on the World Trade Center and other US targets on September 11, 2001, responsibility for which was claimed by Al-Qaeda, a global Islamist terrorist group founded in 1989 – the very year of the political transformations with which modern globalization began. It was not clear, at the time of the attacks or indeed afterward, what exactly the object of the assault was. Such terrorism was interpreted in general terms by the American President George W. Bush as an attack by "enemies of freedom," but in his address to the nation on September 20 he also outlined an account of the ideological basis of the Islamicist position, which was "to disrupt and end a way of life," that is the western way of life in all its political and economic forms. The most radical version of the society that Islamists seek to establish was reflected in practice in the policy of the Taliban in Afghanistan: as Bush put it, "Women are not allowed to attend school. You can be jailed for owning a television. Religion can be practiced only as their leaders dictate."[5] While the patriarchal and religious values of Islamism described here are well publicized, Bush's second sentence "you can be jailed for owning a television" alludes to another feature of Islamism, namely its rejection of western technology with respect to images in particular. While a machine gun, phone, or even the radio may be allowed, all technology involving images, such as television, film, photography, and most forms of the Internet, may be proscribed: societies in which these things are deliberately and self-consciously refused can be encountered all over Asia, from the Lebanon to India, and not just where Islamist regimes are in control. In general, Islamism involves a rejection of ever-increasing wealth and material well-being as the goal of society, in favor of a way of life that focuses on the practice of its own spiritual values. Why should that be such an unthinkable choice for societies to make? Why should people not seek an alternative to the fate of those living in the West – to be "a consumer?" Or, for many of those outside the West, why should they not seek an alternative to living a wasted life as one of the outcasts of Modernity (Bauman 2004)?

The move toward a different kind of state from those on offer from either the West or the communist bloc was anticipated in the creation of the non-aligned movement during the Cold War in 1961. In practice it proved difficult to find a distinctive third way between capitalism and socialism. It would come eighteen years later in the shape of a very different response to western and eastern control: the Islamic religious resurgence signaled by the outcome of the popular Iranian Revolution of 1979, in which the pro-western Shah of Iran was deposed in favor of an Islamic republic. The contemporary idea of an Islamic state is in fact a relatively new one and another anticolonial legacy: it was invented in the 1940s by the British Indian (later Pakistani) Muslim theologian Abul A'la Maududi (1903–79), the founder of the Jamaat-e-Islami party, to offer a third way for decolonized Muslim states, distinct from capitalism and socialism, based on Islamic principles that extend from law to economics (Devji 2013: 228–240). As a model of government it represents a compromise between secular democracy and a theocratic Islamic state, such as existed under the Caliphate and of the kind which contemporary radical Sunni Islamists are trying to recreate. So Iran, while incorporating Sharia law as the basis of its legal system, and with an Islamic cleric as its supreme leader (the "Grand Jurist of Iran"), also has regular elections and a parliament. Although demonized by western politicians, as an Islamic republic Iran could be said to occupy a relatively moderate position within the full political spectrum of the contemporary Middle East. Islam as such in general does not abjure materiality; in his early years, the prophet Muhammad himself participated in an earlier form of a globalized economy, trading goods through Syria between the Mediterranean and the Indian Ocean. Most Muslim states today form an integral part of the global capitalist system. But their often dynastic rule, evident material opulence, and lack of concern for the poor are rejected by radical Islamists, whose various groups represent an opposition not only to the West but also to other forms of Islam, both Shi'a and Sunni. Saudi Arabia, having for many years generously funded institutions all over the world to promote its own strict version of Sunni Islam (Salafism or Wahhabism), has found that it has spawned more radical, oppositional movements that challenge its own: Osama bin Laden, as well as fifteen of the nineteen 9/11 hijackers, were all Saudi nationals. The West's response, involving military intervention in Afghanistan and Iraq in order to institute forms of western democracy, has served only to increase sectarian conflict in the region, particularly between Sunnis and Shi'as, and to have radicalized Islamists even further. Despite their economic, military, and technological superiority, western countries seem relatively powerless in the face of widespread Islamist resistance, which now operates across a broad swathe of the world from West Africa to China.

While the objectives of Al-Qaeda and related groups are expressed and interpreted differently by particular individuals, radical Islamism could be said to form an opposition to globalization, regarded as western, and a desire to create a living space outside its reach. This correlates with the general aim of forcing western powers to withdraw from what are described as the lands of Islam, that is, the territory of the Middle East, and reestablishing the Caliphate that was abolished in 1924 by the secularist Turkish leader Kemal Atatürk (ironically as a result of an intervention by an Indian Khilafat activist designed to protect it). Islamist opposition takes the form of resisting the global modern economic and political system as such, in favor of an alternative way of life that eschews the comforts, liberal ethos, and priorities of capitalist modernity. Islamism in the Middle East has impacted not only politically and socially, but also on economic growth and development in the region. Islamism also draws on some of the older ideas of Islamists and Pan-Islamists in the period of anticolonial movements such as Jamal ad-Din al-Afghani (1838–97), but has adapted its opposition to challenge the contemporary socioeconomic–political organization of the Middle East that forms colonialism's long-term legacy. Perhaps here globalization has encountered its limit after all.

Planetarity

What have been the positive effects of globalization for humanity rather than for corporations? One consequence has been to empower minorities, such as indigenous and tribal peoples, who are more easily able to link together to fight in the international arena for their rights and against the power of corporations practicing resource extraction in their homelands. The values of such people whose lives are much more attuned to working with nature rather than seeking to overcome it through industrialization correlate closely with those of the ecological movements that have developed strongly in the twenty-first century, fronted by international charities such as Friends of the Earth. The very quality that made native people appear less than human in previous centuries – "that they behaved like a part of nature," as Hannah Arendt put it – now makes them seem the most human (Arendt 1958: 192). Globalization, by showing the interconnectedness of societies with respect to the earth on which we all live, has brought with it a much greater awareness of the fact that as human beings we share the planet with many other beings and natural processes, and that we all live within complex and delicately balanced ecological systems that sustain life on earth.

Along with the development of global markets, the exploitation of the earth's resources (its people and its materials) has been a central characteristic of the expansion of capitalism since the nineteenth century. Resistance to colonialism has always been linked to opposition to the forms of abuse and mistreatment that capitalism has utilized for its purposes of resource extraction. While socialism and anticolonial movements have constituted primary forms of challenge, since the beginning of the twentieth century it has also become increasingly clear that the situation of the world's populations cannot improve if their relation to their own environments is ignored. The idea of what Gayatri Chakravorty Spivak (2003) has characterized as "planetarity," or Paul Gilroy (2010) as "planetary consciousness," has gained traction as a way of thinking about the extent to which human beings – instead of being an entirely separate entity in control of nature and the world – are in fact merely one element in its total ecology. What does the world look like if we consider humans as simply a part of the global ecosystem? How far is human activity changing or destroying it? While, for many years, those on the right were skeptical about the importance of environmental issues, highlighted by the refusal of the United States to sign the Kyoto protocol on climate change of 1997, the onset of the effects of global warming far sooner than anticipated in the twenty-first century has urgently increased awareness of humankind's role in what has been called the "Anthropocene" – the geological era in which human beings began to impact significantly upon the ecology of the planet on which they live. These consequences have become increasingly dangerous, such that if uncontained and uncontrolled, the actions of human beings will come to threaten not just, as in the past, particular groups of human beings, but our own survival as a species. Against the violence of human encroachment, diversity, not homogeneity, has been shown to be the way in which evolution has developed successfully: the problem turns out to be the destruction of the ecological environment as part of the colonization of the planet by humankind. The fungus that has still to be found growing on treetops in the as-yet uncleared Amazon rainforest may one day save your child's life.

While humans in general are to blame, there are also issues of international class difference and the priorities of the powerful. As Rob Nixon has shown in *Slow Violence and the Environmentalism of the Poor* (2011), on the one hand there is the problem that environmental damage, though sometimes catastrophic, for the most part works on an invisible timeframe that does not fit our usual forms of narrative representation, the punctuations of sudden events that constitute "news" (compare Gandhi's observation that history "is a record of an interruption of the course of nature"; 1997: 90); on the other hand, the people who are suffering first, and most, are the poor of the world, particularly in the global South, where environmental issues do not figure highly in the priorities of governments. In fact such regimes are more likely to accept the western world's toxic waste, or toxic industries, in return for small financial inducements. The poor of the South, however, have been at the forefront of what Nixon calls "resource insurrections" (Nixon 2011: 5) of the environmental justice movements, because they are closest to the processes of environmental transformation and suffer none of the romanticism of some green movements in the West. As the world becomes increasingly urban, city dwellers grow more and more distant from the fundamental natural processes that ensure human survival. Human dependence on technology, governed by processes that most people do not understand and are incapable of producing themselves, creates a situation of dependency in which their own existence becomes potentially more and more precarious. Weather patterns, rainfall, seasonal temperatures, and sea levels are all changing, so that the earth, on which we live and which sustains us all, is becoming less predictable, less hospitable, and less inhabitable. If globalization represents capitalism's new form of economic imperialism, then that imperialism's ultimate enemy and undoing may turn out to be not human beings but the earth itself.

Notes

1   The Asante Ewer, Museum no 1896,0727.1. http://www.britishmuseum. org/research/collection_online/collection_object_details.aspx? objectId=43862&partId=1.

2   Of the world's seven billion people, six billion have access to mobile phones, but only four and a half billion have access to working toilets. http://www. un.org/apps/news/story.asp?NewsID=44452&Cr=sanitation&Cr1=#. VFPgPvldVnH.

3   For the United States, see the Bailout Tracker at http://www.projects. propublica.org/bailout/.

4   www.hrw.org.

5   http://www.washingtonpost.com/wp-srv/nation/specials/attacked/ transcripts/bushaddress_092001.html.

11

Postcolony

Although the singular term "postcolony" has become widely used, postcolonies are nothing if not diverse. The majority of today's two hundred or so nation-states are former colonies of one kind or another. During the last five hundred years, most were once colonies of just thirteen countries, some of which are themselves former colonies or were themselves colonized in the course of time: Britain, France, Denmark, Holland, Sweden, Belgium, Germany, Spain, Portugal, Italy, Japan, Russia, and the United States. The majority of the remaining states that today make up the world's community of nations are therefore "postcolonies," in the sense of former colonies.

Within the world system of nation-states, the bulk of postcolonies belong to what is known as the global South, a term that has generally replaced the older characterization of "third world" which was problematic, not least when the second world (the communist bloc) disappeared. The third world or global South contains an extraordinary diversity of countries: some of them have operated in some way as a state for hundreds or even thousands of years, others just for decades. This gives them very different degrees of cultural cohesion, tradition, and, inevitably, wealth. The global South includes both the richest country in the world (Qatar) and the poorest (Democratic Republic of the Congo). Other southern nations at the top of the average income scale (measured by Gross National Income [GNI]

Empire, Colony, Postcolony, First Edition. Robert J. C. Young.
© 2015 Robert J. C. Young. Published 2015 by John Wiley & Sons, Ltd.

which may hide great disparities of wealth) include Bermuda, Brunei, Kuwait, Singapore, and UAE (plus Hong Kong and Macau, now special regions of China). However, the list of richest and poorest countries remains dominated at the top end by Europe and North America and by Africa at the bottom. The economic disparity between the nation-states of the world amounts in effect to an unregulated global system of inequality – as Kiran Desai puts it in *The Inheritance of Loss*, "Profit could only be harvested in the gap between nations, working one against the other" (Desai 2006: 205). This disparity falls with a particular burden upon many a postcolony, unless it has been blessed with natural resources such as oil – though in some cases, as in Nigeria, this can also be considered a curse. At their most challenging, the characteristics of the underprivileged postcolonial states may include poverty, corruption within the political and legal system, lack of policing and high crime rates, and absence of health provision. The scarcely functioning economy may be largely sustained by remittances from nationals who have left the country to work abroad. At a political level, postcolonies in such a state will rarely operate according to democratic principles.

In this world of unequal states, what difference though does having once been a colony make to a country? Is it meaningful to remember or has it become irrelevant in today's globalized world? Does it make any sense to put such a diverse group of countries together? We could say that there are fundamentally three kinds of postcolony: those countries that were once colonies, *former colonies*, followed by two kinds of former colonies with special characteristics: former settler colonies that are now *settler postcolonies*, and those that are somehow still functioning as ex-colonies, which might be called unfinished or *dysfunctional postcolonies*. With respect to the first, more general category, we can think of the postcolony in terms of understanding persisting colonial effects that continue to play themselves out in former colonies, even if they are underlying features that are normally assumed as an everyday fact of life, as just the way things are – the legal system, the educational system, or the presence of indigenous people, for example. These involve the historical conditions that follow from having once been a colony, or a colonizer. They may be structural or cultural features of the country, or they may be historical oddities: Sweden only abolished its annual payment to the King to compensate for his loss of a one-year ownership (1813–14) of the island of Guadeloupe in 1983. Or it may form part of a historical memory that continues to have significant political currency: the ideology of liberty in the United States, for example, is closely linked to the historical narrative of its declaration of independence in 1776.

If colonial history is the nightmare from which every colony seeks to awake to a state of freedom and autonomy, by the twenty-first century most colonies could be said to be fairly fully awake: for them, colonialism at this point constitutes their historical legacy. These are the postcolonies that are simply former colonies, that have, to invoke the work of Michel Foucault (2003), managed to create successfully the sovereign state machine of modernity.

The United States, however, properly belongs to the kind of postcolony that can be described as former settler colonies. The settler postcolony will share the general characteristics of former colonies, but with one additional feature, awkwardly persisting into the present: the presence of indigenous people, as a distinct group who have survived the history of settlement but live on as a minority in a country which they do not control.

The third way to think about the postcolony is with respect to those countries which do not seem to have fully transitioned from their colonial formation, that are still dominated by conditions arising from a colonial inheritance that they have been unable to transcend in order to achieve the situation of a stable society – postcolonies that remain or have become dysfunctional. This is how the African philosopher Achille Mbembe has used the term, a usage that will be explored in the last part of this chapter. The three different kinds of postcolony will now be described in more detail. We will begin with the question of colonial remains in the former colony: since all postcolonies are of course former colonies, some of their individual characteristics (law or language, for example) will be common to many. The difference of the postcolony as former colony from the other kinds of postcolony comes with the absence of a large settler population, and its ability to function fully as a modern state.

The Postcolony as Former Colony

A country's sovereign existence as a state, and any claim to be a nation-state, is itself a product of the international system of nation-states that emerged as a legacy of European nationalism, anticolonial nationalism, and imperial world war. There is nothing inevitable about the political organization of the nation-state: historically, there have been many other types of country or territory and in the future it is likely that others will emerge. Moreover the nation-state as a political entity has itself changed. In its formation, the modern postcolony was in a fundamentally different position from the European nation-state: it could not create itself as a nation through acquiring colonies abroad. Rather than evolving over centuries, it was probably instituted ready-made by the colonial power at the stroke of the midnight hour. The constitution and political system were likely drawn up by the civil servants of the departing colonizer; the apparatus of government and civil governance, the bureaucracy, the system of law, the army, and the police that the new independent state took over were not its own but those that had been fashioned by the colonial regime. At inception, the postcolony then had to operate according to the international environment to which states have to conform, organized by a host of international laws on sovereignty, trade, foreign investment, and exchange which have already been set up by the former imperial powers.

At independence, power was often handed over to a nationalist elite. Some postcolonies exist in a state of permanent tension: between the middle and upper classes, who are educated, secular and westernized, and the lower classes and poor, who are less educated and more religious. Such countries have to negotiate the political pressure between the forms of the state that these different constituencies demand, for example between a westernized secular democracy receptive to the demands of international capitalism and a communist (during the Cold War) or (latterly) a theocratic state. Postcolonial states have often been criticized by those in the West for their political instability. But it is astonishing that having been ruled as colonial autocracies, with a population that may have scarcely ever voted except in the run-up to independence, they were then suddenly expected to behave as mature democracies overnight. It is not so surprising that a number of postcolonial states have lurched back at times into various forms of autocracy when that was the historical colonial form that had been used to run the country for so long.

Ethnic Diversity

Along with the form of political sovereignty, the arbitrary boundaries of the state may correspond to old colonial divisions made with little respect for local nations, ethnic formations, or cultural and religious practices of the people living in those areas. Examples of illogical and unstable borders abound in Africa in particular, but can also be found in South Asia (for example, the arbitrary Durand line of 1896 that still constitutes the porous, contested boundary between Pakistan and Afghanistan). Iraq or Nigeria would be examples of countries made up of challenging groups of heterogeneous peoples who would likely never have chosen of themselves to constitute a single state together. The problem of the postcolony therefore is that its ethnic groups, languages, cultures, and often its religions are frequently multiple, and do not conform to the original European model of the consolidated nation-state which had been carefully crafted over an extended period of time. Speakers of different languages will often see themselves as belonging to different ethnicities, as people with a whole set of distinct cultural values. They may well have been there for centuries or millennia, so there is nothing postcolonial about the fact of their existence. However, they will now encounter the situation and conditions of the postcolony's existence as a diversified state, often characterized, as a result, by factional strife based on ethnic or religious differences.

Looking to the European models of nation-states, the governments of decolonized states often pursue a nationalist agenda of homogenization as a way of "nation building," just as the European Union itself now spends millions of Euros to encourage a sense of Europeanness among its nations. In practice, nation building can function as a euphemism for repressing ethnic minorities and limiting their freedoms, particularly if they seem to have a different history, or worse, religion, from the mainstream. A simple but clear indication of this process comes with the enforcement of one language as the official language in a multilingual state. The imposition of Urdu as the common language of East and West Pakistan was a major factor in the revolt of West Pakistan, which became the separate country of Bangladesh in 1971. The enforcement of Sinhala as the only official language of Ceylon (Sri Lanka) with the Sinhala Only Act of 1956 was widely regarded by the Tamil minority as symptomatic of a supremacist Sinhalese agenda and led to fifty years of civil war. In the situation where a province has sought independence where territories were contiguous, repression of a break-away state has largely been enforced militarily, as in Sri Lanka, in Indian-administered Kashmir and the Northeastern provinces of India, or Katanga or Biafra in Africa. Military defeat and reassertion of authority by the government does not generally resolve the issues that generated the underlying conflict, as in the defeat of the Igbo people in Nigeria in 1970, or the Tamils in Sri Lanka in 2009. In an interesting resurfacing of precolonial remains, in the twenty-first century the Islamist militant group Boko Harām have taken control of many of the Northeastern provinces of Nigeria, in the area of the former Bornu Empire which had lasted from 1380 to 1893, when it was annexed by the British.

Law, Education, and Language

It might be argued that the deepest legacy of colonial rule on any postcolony is the legal system (Benton 2010; Kirkby and Coleborne 2001). The spread of particular legal traditions established one important basis for globalization: as a result of empire and colonization, there are broadly three legal systems at work in the world today – the Napoleonic civil code, British common law, and Muslim law as practiced in the Abbasid Caliphate and the Ottoman and Mughal empires. The Code Napoléon became the benchmark of codified civil law in Europe and, by means of the French Empire, eventually a large part of the rest of the world. The United States, reflecting its origins (in part) as British and French colonies, duly uses both the Napoleonic civil code and British common law. Muslim law remains today in many formerly Ottoman or Muslim countries, such as Bangladesh, Greece, Egypt, India, Iran, Iraq, Israel, Jordan, Lebanon, Pakistan, Palestine, Syria, and even Greece, which in almost every other respect has purged the memory of its four-hundred-year Ottoman rule from its culture as if it had never happened.

Many of the cultural differences between states are also founded on their different forms of education. As with the law, so, too, educational systems are often the inheritance of colonial institutions; not merely the institutions themselves, but the very modes and methods of education – even the language in which education is conducted (Pietsch 2013). The founding of universities was hardly an immediate priority for most colonizers, except for those in the Americas: the Spanish established universities throughout their South American colonies from the sixteenth century. Harvard University in the United States was founded in 1636, old enough, according to a widespread (but most probably inaccurate) rumor, to have offered a job to Galileo. Elsewhere, universities were set up in the later periods of colonialism, often, as with the University of the West Indies (founded in 1948), with coming independence in mind. While the origins of the university (though not the term) date back to Islamic cultures – the earliest degree-granting institution is generally accorded to the University of Karueein, a madrasa founded in 859 in Morocco by a woman, Fatima al-Fihri – the modern university is essentially a western construction. This has facilitated its speedy transformation since the late twentieth century into a globalized system whose universal language is English, a neoliberal structure in which the university's primary function has become not so much the pursuit of knowledge but to compete with other universities.

As the increasing ubiquity of English as the language of the world's universities might suggest, the most obvious and ubiquitous colonial legacy of all is that of language. Although there are a few examples of postcolonies where the colonial language has almost disappeared (French in Vietnam, for example), for the most part colonies continue to a greater or lesser extent to utilize the language of colonial rule, and this is reflected in the list of major world languages. Even in a country like Namibia, which ceased to be a German colony in 1915, German is still widely spoken; Italian is still spoken in the Dodecanese Islands and in Somalia. In settler colonies, the colonial language dominates: Spanish, along with Portuguese, is the primary language as well as the basis of the name "Latin" America, while English rests supreme in North America, even if increasingly it vies with Spanish, which has effectively become the language of the underclass. In Africa, at least one of the official languages of most states will be English, French, or Portuguese, while English remains the widely spoken non-native language of South Asia. To attend an English-medium school is the aspiration of every upper-class or upwardly mobile child (or rather parent) in India. While in Europe for the most part a national language was successfully established in the eighteenth and nineteenth centuries through the suppression of minor languages and dialects, most postcolonial states are multilingual and rarely have a single national language in place that can be shared equitably by all. As has been suggested, language, which often grounds the basis of ethnic identity, has as a result been a primary site of conflict in many postcolonial states. Even if formerly the language of the colonizer, an international language such as English or French can serve as a useful, now relatively neutral, alternative that avoids the dominance of the language of one particular local group, which is why they remain the official language of many postcolonial states.

Ethnic diversity, law, education, language: a former colony like Singapore offers a perfect example of continuity between colonial and postcolonial states in its conditions, institutions, and practices. It also happens to have become one of the richest countries in the world – unhindered, or alternatively facilitated, by its colonial past.

The Settler Postcolony

The most politically stable postcolonial states have often been former settler colonies in the Americas and Oceania peopled by immigrant Europeans whose culture and religion had evolved together over centuries. The postcoloniality of such states is marked by one significant element: the presence of indigenous peoples. This is what makes them "settler postcolonies." Many of those countries today might not choose to regard themselves as postcolonies, but one defining marker of the former settler colony continues to haunt them: a different presence, the continued, marked, population of original pre-settler inhabitants, indigenous populations who are sometimes characterized with the term "fourth world." The social and political discrepancy between the general population made up of immigrants and those descended from former settlers and indigenous peoples is a feature of almost all such states, from Canada to Chile. The degree of mixed populations varies considerably, but even in a country like Mexico there is still a division between the *mestizaje* and indigenous population. It is in these postcolonies that the political issues surrounding indigeneity are most evident, resulting from a discrepancy between a majority, relatively prosperous population of settler origin, and indigenous peoples whose lands have been historically appropriated.

The historical experience of indigenous people in settler colonies has often been one of attempted genocide (Moses 2008). The best-known example of colonial genocide is that of the Herero and Namakwa people in German Southwest Africa (Namibia) in 1904–7. As Kurtz's scrawled note "Exterminate all the brutes!" at the end of Conrad's *Heart of Darkness* (1899) may suggest, the word "exterminate" was freely used by Europeans with respect to native populations in the nineteenth century, and by no means only with reference to the past. Native Americans in the Americas were eliminated by the millions after the arrival of the Spanish and the English through a combination of war, disease, and persecution (Stannard 1992; Alvarez 2014); in the nineteenth and early twentieth centuries, independent Argentina followed a deliberate policy of "invisiblization" for its native population and their cultures (Delrio et al. 2010); at one point, Australia sought to breed out the blackness of its aboriginal peoples according to a state eugenics program.[1] The politics of guilt and restitution that this history produces creates a fundamental difference from the many places elsewhere on the world's main landmass where indigenous groups with separate identities live distinct from the main population. In the postcolonial settler colony their status is very different, since the indigenous people are the "first nations" who were there before the settlers arrived (Coates 2004; Smith 1998).

The settler postcolonies of North and South America, and of Oceania, will therefore always have a particular identity that keeps their postcolonial status in the foreground. In general, as has been stated, when such colonies achieved independence it was the settlers who assumed control, and continued their own colonial rule over indigenous peoples. These "fourth world" people remained largely unregarded until the late twentieth century when indigenous groups successfully developed political and legal strategies that forced their governments to take heed of them.

The Postcolony as a Zone of Dysfunction

The last kind of postcolony, the *dysfunctional postcolony*, comprises the former colony where historical colonial rule continues to be played out as a kind of unresolved, unfinished business, where the colonial legacy disrupts the workings of the state. It was in this sense that the term "postcolony" was first brought into widespread academic use around 1990 by the political philosopher Achille Mbembe (Mbembe 1990: 21). Mbembe's work began with an initial focus on his own country of origin, Cameroon, a postcolonial African state made up from parts of the former colonies of British, French, and German Cameroons. First occupied by the French in the late nineteenth century, it became independent in 1960. "The notion 'postcolony,'" Mbembe argued, "simply refers to the specific identity of a given historical trajectory: that of societies recently emerging from the experience of colonization." It soon became clear, however, that Mbembe's postcolony names not the recent postcolonial state as such but a particular form that it takes in sub-Saharan Africa, in states such as Cameroon which are controlled by those who govern them through a combination of ostentatious display and brutality (Mbembe 1992a: 2, 1992b). Mbembe's postcolony, therefore, is not a general description of all former colonies, but of former colonies that operate according to specific dysfunctional modes of domination and violence. Such states, according to Mbembe, through their bureaucracies and institutions create not only their own sense of the world but also the social environment in which these become real: they produce the limit of what is both possible and permissible to think. To go beyond these is to incur the operation of pain and death. The combination of authoritarian display with corruption obliges their populations to participate in the performance of the state in order to survive. This means that the customary political binaries of domination and opposition, of power and resistance, fail to describe the way in which the inhabitants of the postcolony are caught up within the terms that the state has laid down.

Instead of the classic colonial dichotomy of collaboration or antagonism, Mbembe argues, the postcolonial relation is marked by a "convivial relation" between authority (*commandement*) and the people: what is distinctive about such states is that power is organized through forms such as spectacle or carnival, by means of which opposition is marginalized (recall the Delhi Durbars of British colonial India). The postcolony becomes a type of often farcical theatre, in which all parties take on mutually constituting roles. Though the population may undo the language and imagery of the state in a carnivalesque inversion, their potential meanings are pluralistic enough for any inversion to be already contained within them. This, Mbembe suggests, produces a "zombification" both of the dominant and those whom they dominate. The question that follows is how the postcolony can ever leave the dark night of post-coloniality within which it dwells (Mbembe 2010). Since there are few legitimate channels for opposition, when resistance does comes it turns swiftly to violence and militarized conflict.

"Kleptocracies" has been a term also used to describe autocratic states with a high level of corruption and appropriation of wealth by the ruling elite, governed by what the French historian Jean-François Bayart has called "the politics of the belly" (Bayart 1993). This describes the ways in which the state sets up a particular kind of culture of patronage, palm-greasing, and dependency, along with ceremonial exhibitionism and together with a general lack of human rights and criminal accountability, as well as violence and exploitation. The kind of state described by Mbembe as the African postcolony would include such countries as Cameroon, the Central African Republic, Congo, Nigeria, Sudan, Togo, and formerly Rwanda (Mamdani 2002). However, corruption by itself is by no means a predominantly African phenomenon: many Southeast Asian, North African, and Middle Eastern countries can be found at the bottom of the "Corruption Perceptions Index" (2012).[2]

Mbembe and Bayart's essays make provocative and original interventions in the political analysis of sub-Saharan African states, moving the argument away from the typical area-studies language of corrupt or failed states that are compared on a "neutral" (i.e., guided by western normative assumptions and criteria) basis with other states of the world. Mbembe's account of the postcolony is, however, somewhat undiscriminating in the generality of its claims, even if his range of reference is exclusively African (though even here, it would not, for example, apply to South Africa). The majority of postcolonies work reasonably well. The dysfunctional postcolony describes specifically those states whose existence seems not to have moved out of that of the postcolonial, in situations where the state still wrestles with the actuality, or the remains, of its colonial experience and legacy. The unfinished, inoperative postcolony has yet to leave the historical fact of colonization behind, existing in an apparent failure or refusal to conform to the normative global model of the sovereign nation. It is the state that has yet to create a stable infrastructure, economy, and civic society that will allow it to compete successfully in the world with other countries according to the neoliberal model. Instead the state is in some sense not fully in control of itself or of its people, in terms of the presence of war, violence, the absence of the institutions and procedures of legality, and of cultural and intellectual production. The dysfunctional postcolony appears to exist in its present form not because it has become a state with its own particular identity, but solely because it was formerly a colonial state. As the relic of a state, it is marked by the absence of autonomy, or perhaps even more so by absence itself. Its economy will largely function "informally," its GDP sustained by remittances from migrants to their families.

What distinguishes the dysfunctional postcolony as a civil state is that instead of stability it generates terror, tumult, instability, an uncertain life for its population: ethnic strife, economic disabilities, absence of infrastructure, the migration and diaspora of its people. The inoperative postcolony has never fully achieved its own political legitimacy or established self-sufficiency after the moment of decolonization. It constitutes a regime that repeats and exacerbates the former colonial situation by ruling according to unmediated violence, a politics of terror, torture and the right to kill, rather than popular consent or through the exercise of the law (Mbembe 2003: 32). The colonial state, its own claims notwithstanding, never achieved legitimacy other than through its exercise and threat of violence: the foundation of violence as the only legitimating force connects the colonial state to that of the dysfunctional postcolony. However, this does not take the form of industrialized killing by the state as exemplified in Nazi modernity. Here the state itself is unworkable, and may have deteriorated to the extent that the regime is merely one of the actors among a cohort of competing militias and armies of local political groups and fiefdoms with diverse claims and objectives, each of which are struggling for control of overlapping areas or particular enclaves that may stretch across national frontiers into other nominal states. They will be mobile and difficult to engage, often retreating into remote border areas for safety. A feature of such militias may be the use of child soldiers, irregular combatants, mercenaries, or seconded military from neighboring states, funded by appropriation of local resources and minerals. Continuing violence and war may not be a simple question of resolvable factional conflict but part of a heterogeneous militia economy where continuing states of emergencies and endemic disorder are advantageous to many of the armed groups involved (Keen 2012). Though such conflictual economies may mimic certain features of civil war, they do not involve civil war in the classic form of a war between two sides contained by state boundaries. To live in the postcolony as the zone of dysfunction is to be in a world where the aim of life encompasses no more than sheer survival.

We can compare the idea of the dysfunctional postcolony as an intermediary form to Hamid Dabashi's argument in his book on the Arab revolutions that began in 2011, *The Arab Spring: The End of Postcolonialism* (Dabashi 2012). Dabashi begins by announcing: "What we are witnessing in what used to be called the 'Middle East' (and beyond) marks the end of postcolonial ideological formations" (xvii). The Arab revolutions have transcended the state of postcoloniality, the autocratic regimes or their inheritors put in place by the European mandate powers in the 1920s and 1930s, in order, Dabashi suggests, "to create a new geography of liberation" (xviii). While the revolutions did indeed open up a modality of popular political participation that reached out far beyond the traditional structures of domination to break, in several cases, the autocratic regime itself, any expectation of a quick transition to democratic process in the Arab states proved to be far too optimistic. There were too many other powerful interests at play, from Al-Qaeda and other competing Islamist groups to repressed nationalisms to sectarian strife to the "Arab Platoons" of Yamas. With very few exceptions such as Tunisia, what has happened instead since 2011 are transformations of these postcolonies into new modalities of the postcolonial as the zone of dysfunction, where autocracy is succeeded by turmoil, where individual groups transmute and coalesce into others, where politics and war become a struggle not for the power of the state, as in classic Leninist revolutionary theory, but for constructing territorial power according to new – or ancient – religious, cultural, and geographical formations. This suggests that the greatest failure in certain respects was indeed by the postcolonial leaders – tyrants, autocrats – of countries such as Libya, Iraq, and Syria. They ruled by fear and failed to create any cohesive infrastructure or identity for their postcolonies, or any stabilizing resource of shared polity. They left behind only unfinished business.

Notes

1 www.stolengenerations.info.
2 The other relevant index here is the Ibrahim Index of African Governance (IIAG).

12

Postcolonialism

What is postcolonialism? Quite simply, it is what Walter Benjamin called "the tradition of the oppressed" (Benjamin 2003: 392). In that sense, it affiliates to other political movements such as Marxism and socialism, feminism, and environmentalism that have fought to challenge dominant power structures of the world. While Marxism specifically emphasizes the power of capitalism and its exploitation of the working class, feminism the power of patriarchy and its exploitation of women, and environmentalism the relentless exploitation of the earth, postcolonialism focuses on the power of first-world nations and their historic exploitation and oppression of the global South. Together these movements critique the oppressions of class, gender, race, and earth. These categories often overlap, and there is little incompatibility among them, more a question of emphasis.

"Postcolonialism" may not be the best term for the challenge to, and analysis of, oppressive forms of western power, and people have often said as much. No one, however, has yet found a better word for the political perspective of the world's oppressed, the damned or wretched of the earth, to cite the famous first line of the *Internationale* – which Frantz Fanon used as the title for his remarkable book (Fanon 1966). The invocation of colonialism may seem to be calling up specters from the past, but in global terms colonialism itself represents the most widespread form of oppression in human history; its harsh

Empire, Colony, Postcolony, First Edition. Robert J. C. Young.
© 2015 Robert J. C. Young. Published 2015 by John Wiley & Sons, Ltd.

power relations have resulted in the word "colonial" becoming a metaphor for the imbalance of power itself. At the same time, the prefix *post* marks and represents the historic achievement of liberation, that moment of reversal, in which, as Christopher Hill put it in describing the English Revolution in the seventeenth century, the world is turned upside down (Hill 1972). The postcolonial represents the perspective of how the world looks from below not from above, from the global South, not from the North. Instead of London, New York, or Moscow, how does the world appear from Bamako, Ramallah, or Santa Cruz de la Sierra? Or from Siriyado, Fuleri, Jaraarwadi, three of the forty-odd villages in Banni, India, that are not even on the map? Or to a migrant from the Ivory Coast as she sits with forty others on a small open boat slowly making its way through rough seas from the Libyan coast toward the Italian island of Lampedusa? Such perspectives are rarely the ones that are presented in the media or in mainstream forms of cultural expression, unless they are presented in documentary form. Within the realm of the postcolonial, the people of the global South are not objects of someone else's understanding but active, speaking subjects, whose knowledge is taken as seriously by others as by themselves as a way of thinking or acting or dealing with the world.

To translate oneself from the perspective of the dominant to that of the subordinated, from being seen as an object to being a subject is the core structural and political move that postcolonialism involves (Young 2003: 138–147). This transformation was the subject of Frantz Fanon's classic *Black Skin, White Masks* (Fanon 1986), one of the first books to analyze the lived experience of a racist colonial society from the point of view of the person of color. In the same way, in *The Wretched of the Earth* (Fanon 1966), offers a historical analysis of colonialism that is set against the subjective knowledge of colonial rule from the point of view of the colonized person. This double perspective accounts for the importance of literature, especially fiction, to postcolonialism, because fiction is the form of writing that can give an account of history at the same time as it shows what it is like for the individuals involved to live through such times, offering subjective accounts of objective processes, putting the psychic into dialogue with the social and the historical. As is also the case for feminism, literature has been one of the few forms of knowledge, of cultural production, where such issues have historically been broached and explored.

The reach of the postcolonial is therefore almost impossibly broad: it can be concerned with everything that matters to the people of the South, wherever they may be, including the global North. For this reason, while it articulates the perspectives of those who live outside, or come from, the world beyond the borders of what has come to be known as "the West," the postcolonial identifies with other political practices that reverse customary power relations in the name of women, the working class, or even the earth itself. This will involve forms of understanding that have developed outside the West, including the non-western understanding of the West itself, the tradition that identifies itself as Southern thought (Cassano 2011).

Knowledge and Theory

At the level of official knowledge produced by the global university system, the postcolonial involves the intrusion of the non-West into the academic realm that was developed in its modern form according to western protocols in the nineteenth century. This involves a certain paradox, since it is difficult to state alternatives within this system without to a certain degree accepting its protocols. The point was made very effectively in 1945 by the French author Antoine de Saint-Exupéry in his classic children's book *The Little Prince*. It is not a coincidence that this story comes in a children's book. As Charles Dickens knew, everyone as a child has some version of one distinctive aspect of what we would now call the postcolonial experience – because as a child, you are looking up at the world, relatively powerless, from below. Here is Saint-Exupéry:

> I have serious reason to believe that the planet from which the little prince came is the asteroid known as B-612.
>
> This asteroid has only once been seen through the telescope. That was by a Turkish astronomer, in 1909.
>
> On making his discovery, the astronomer had presented it to the International Astronomical Congress, in a great demonstration. But he was in Turkish costume, and so nobody would believe what he said.

Grown-ups are like that …

Fortunately, however, for the reputation of Asteroid B-612, a Turkish dictator [Kemal Atatürk] made a law that his subjects, under pain of death, should change to European costume. So in 1920 the astronomer gave his demonstration over again, dressed with impressive style and elegance. And this time everybody accepted the report. (de Saint-Exupéry 1945: 15)

Saint Exupéry's story suggests that within academia, even in science, you have to conform to certain western cultural as well as scientific conventions in order to be heard and believed. In general, however, at the level of science, there are certain conditions and procedures, such as the elimination of variables other than the one you are studying, or repeatability, that have become acknowledged as standard procedure to which any credible form of science is going to have to conform. As knowledge, science operates as a universal, though this does not mean that it is not subject to politics and economics in terms of its practices and priorities: a postcolonial understanding of science has developed in areas such as economics or ecology where social values form part of the understanding. In the knowledge produced by the social sciences and even more the humanities, on the other hand, no such universal procedures exist in the same way. What is employed instead is a recognized "methodology" which sets the parameters of the investigation or discussion. While this is typically made explicit in the social sciences, in the humanities, for example in the study of literary texts, such methodology is often left implicit – it is up to the reader to work out what assumptions are being made. Postcolonialism is concerned with the grounds of knowledge – epistemology – because it argues that such positions are often either unwittingly ethnocentric or Eurocentric, or both. In order to think through the possibilities of a different kind of knowledge, those working from a postcolonial perspective have therefore tended to develop self-consciously their own specific modes of understanding and to explore the ways in which these differ from the norm. This is sometimes given the name "theory."

Such theory is not theory in the scientific sense outlined above. It rather represents a way of trying to reconceptualize our forms of understanding. This sort of thinking is more philosophical and inevitably does not appeal to everyone, even within the academy. But it can be useful in helping to think otherwise, outside the norm of the dominant group. The way to approach postcolonial theory is not to imagine that it is some complete system that has been totally thought out and which you have to master. In fact the self-assurance that comes with the idea of mastering and masterful knowledge, fundamental to western thinking, is one of the things that are under challenge. Postcolonial theory is a set of concepts and ideas that are designed to be provocative, and to make people think differently, particularly about things that they thought they already knew about. It is proactive rather than comprehensive, total, or complete. "Postcolonial theory" involves a set of interrelated concerns and concepts that relate to each other rather like the different areas of a Venn diagram which overlap in one common area but for the most part pursue their own objective. If one of these interests you, others less so, that is the right reaction.

Rather than try to summarize them as if they form a totality, therefore, in the rest of this chapter I shall discuss some of the most important areas of concern that are articulated within postcolonial studies. They make up a cluster of issues, which are at once theoretical, aesthetic, and political. The politics of postcolonialism, the tradition of the oppressed, undergirds them all and provides the rationale for their inclusion.

Orientalism

The underlying concern of postcolonialism involves a politics of knowledge. This was the focus of the book that initiated postcolonial studies in its modern form: Edward W. Said's *Orientalism: Western Representations of the Orient* (1978). In this book, Said claimed that westerners had, over the course of the past five hundred years, developed a certain view of what they called "the Orient," that is the Near and Far East, that involved a homogeneous tradition across many different forms of writing, from travel writing to political science, from history to fiction to area studies. Though separated according to their disciplines, or their national origins, all such writers, Said argued, projected a common representation of the East. The problem with it, he suggested, was that it was not based on reality but on western preconceptions and stereotypes, transmitted from one book to the other, with the result that its image of the East and of eastern peoples ended up being more about the West and its fantasies of "otherness" than the lands and people that it claimed to describe. Such knowledge was essentially false or at the very least partial knowledge. Nevertheless it was employed as knowledge within the mechanisms of rule and control that made up western imperial power over the East, and indeed latterly was constructed in order to facilitate this. Such was the determining power of the economic, political, and social forces that drove Orientalism, Said maintained, that no one, not even radical critics such as Karl Marx, could escape it. Despite decolonization, Said suggested that such processes continue today. This sweeping thesis offended a lot of people, particularly academics in western universities who had dedicated their lives to the study of eastern cultures. It was indeed problematic in the totality of its determinism, which allowed for relatively little nuance or differentiation – Orientalism was a paradigm from which no one could escape. Said's thesis came across not only as a form of critique but also as an accusation. Yet, if so, it hit a profound chord with those in other situations of apparent powerlessness or disempowerment around the world. Said was a Palestinian who had lived his life through the experience of a people whose political claims, and perspectives on their experience of dispossession, had for the most part been blithely disregarded by the great powers of the world. In critiquing Orientalism, Said was protesting against his own fate and that of his nation.

"Orientalism" represented a contemporary form of anticolonial cultural and political critique. Its importance went beyond the remit of its own particular focus, broad as that was, because Said had put his finger on an important issue that has already been outlined, namely that knowledge, which is assumed to be objective in order to be proper knowledge, is often not objective at all but full of cultural prejudice. It is easier to see and accept this when looking at knowledge of the past – for example, the many books about race or phrenology that were published in the nineteenth century – than to be aware of the limits of one's own preconceptions in the present. This produces a situation where it is easy to criticize writers of previous eras because their thinking does not conform to ours today, without an equal reflection on the fact that we are all, to some degree, products of our own time. No one can completely step outside the thinking and assumptions of their own era. Arguably, therefore, once the obvious forms of critique have been gone through in order to highlight the limitations of the thought of others, whether in the present or the past, it is more constructive to focus on what was radical and transformative about them – especially in relation to our own preconceptions and assumptions. Once we have noted the presence of generic racist attitudes typical of its period in Conrad's *Heart of Darkness* (1902), for example, the more interesting question becomes how far did Conrad challenge other assumptions that would have been held by his contemporary readers – and how far does he contest those that we hold today? Why does this novella seem to speak to us today so profoundly when in earlier decades it was seen as less important?

Culture

The corollary to Said's project in *Orientalism*, from which postcolonial studies begins, is to rethink knowledge, of culture, or history, or literature, according to protocols that do not enforce partial or Eurocentric assumptions. One aspect of this will be to rethink the concept of culture itself (a relatively recent invention), particularly its division in many parts of the world into the duality of high culture and popular culture. How far does popular culture, designated as less important, amount not merely to different forms of pleasure and expression but also to resistance to power and its hierarchies of value? In the terms of the Russian literary critic Mikhail Bakhtin, popular culture can be thought of as representing a perpetual carnival in which forms of authority endorsed by high culture are continuously challenged and overthrown (Bakhtin 1968; Stallybrass and White 1986). Culture as a concept in Europe, it has been suggested, was originally invented at the end of the eighteenth century as a way of formulating, and producing, the elusive totality of the nation. To that end, its function was to bring the different elements of the people into the harmonious resolution of the nation itself. European popular culture, however, was never so fully engaged in this ideological project. In the twentieth century, the structure underwent something of a reversal: while popular culture was appropriated by the commercial media, high art, that is, unpopular culture, became more concerned to challenge that commercialization and commodification of everyday life by emphasizing fragmentation and unassimilability. Toward the end of the twentieth century, culture began to be employed on a different conceptual project, to combat racism and ethnocentric attitudes, and to create a "third space" of inclusion for ethnic minorities and cultural difference within the nation. This is the project of Zadie Smith's novel *White Teeth* (2000), which critiques the identity politics of multiculturalism for a more syncretic account of ethnicities and cultures, with its characters engaged in permanent acts of cultural translation. In the same way, postcolonial studies challenged Eurocentric academic traditions, for example, the idea of the nation as culturally or ethnically homogeneous, while advocating its hybridity instead (Bhabha 1994).

One of the wider effects of postcolonial studies in the literary field has been to challenge the dominance of the western literary canon. This has been evident in the popularity of contemporary international novelists as well as in the resurgence of interest in World Literature. First proposed by Goethe at the beginning of the nineteenth century, endorsed by Marx and Engels in the *Communist Manifesto*, revived at the end of the nineteenth, and then again at the end of the twentieth century, World Literature seeks to do away with the idea that there are a small number of (European) literatures of high value, and a large number that are minor by comparison. Instead, it offers an equitable framework for considering all literatures of the world side by side, without prior presumptions (Casanova 2004; Damrosch 2003; Lazarus 2011). For many, World Literature is also attractive because it offers a way of getting away from the nationalistic division of literatures organized according to the countries in which they were written. In earlier times, the division was made more equitably, that is according to the languages in which literatures were written (Greek, Roman, Italian, French, English, Spanish, German), but by the nineteenth century, with the identification of language with nation, this linguistic literary division had become a national one. World literature once again allows the linguistic fabric of the literary work to be foregrounded. In practice, of course, no one can speak or read every language on earth, so much

World Literature is read in translation. Since it is most widely taught in the United States, followed by the Hispanic countries, it might seem that it also runs the risk of English absorbing all the literatures of the world. But this is only how it looks from the United States. From Buenos Aires, or Paris, Tokyo, or Tianjin, World Literature looks very different. Since it is a sphere, no one can have a total perspective on the world at one time, and the same is true for its literatures. One problem may be that the very concept of literature is a recent one, once again associated with the development in Europe of literature as an academic subject. What counts as "literature" can well be a matter for serious debate. For example, many anthologies of World Literature in English include extracts from the Bible and the Quran, included alongside, say, some of the poems of e.e. cummings, oblivious of the fact that for billions of people on earth, these sacred texts have a very different function and truth value altogether. For them, they are not literature in the modern secular sense.

A different way of interrogating hierarchies of value with respect to literature and culture would be in relation to the French sociologist Pierre Bourdieu's concept of "cultural capital" (Bourdieu 1984). Every society on earth produces forms of culture, but not all these cultures are evaluated side by side. In the nineteenth century the cultures of the world were separated into the civilized and the primitive. Sailors, missionaries, and travelers with experience of the latter wrote accounts of them that were then studied under the name of "anthropology" in Europe. It was not until the end of the century that it occurred to Europeans to perform an anthropology of their own culture, an activity that they named sociology. Both disciplines concurred in the elimination of history, the first because it was considered that primitive people had no history, by definition their primitiveness put them out of historical time, and in the second because the idea was to see how society functioned synchronically in the present. This synchronicity enabled structuralists to propose a method according to which all the languages and cultures of the world could be studied together in the same way, without any imperialist hierarchy of value. That hierarchy of civilized and primitive had been equally applied within Europe with respect to the difference between high and popular culture (popular culture preserving a link to "ethnic" or "folk" cultures). Bourdieu conceived of this difference in terms of what he called cultural capital, on an analogy with financial capital: some cultures, such as that of the French middle and upper classes, had accrued a lot of capital and therefore status, others (of the working class, or colonized Algerians) were deemed to have none at all. With cultural capital comes prestige, status, and even identity – all of them entities that are in different ways political. The question then became, how does cultural capital get generated? The answer obviously is through cultural production, but through cultural production that will be recognized globally as "culture" that has value. Creating exquisite blow-pipes may be charming but will only create cultural capital at the lowest level, items for the ethnographic museum. Even at its most positive, "primitive" culture is only seen as of value to the degree that it restores the culture of the West. This is brought out in Alejo Carpentier's famous 1953 novel, *The Lost Steps* (Carpentier 2001). The narrator, a composer, flees the anomie and superficiality of New York to go on an expedition to the Amazon to find primitive instruments for a museum to prove his thesis about the origin of music; when he reaches a primordial village deep in the jungle where he feels he wants to live forever, his own creative block is released and he begins writing a Cantata – that could only be performed back in New York.

The desire for cultural capital explains why countries all over the world bid to stage the Olympics or the World Cup, even though these events may be ruinous in financial terms. It gives them prestige and recognition, and with these comes power and influence. It also generates an increased sense of a secure identity, which is why anticolonial struggles typically start out with trying to generate cultural capital through their own cultural production: the anticolonial movements were fought not just on the streets and in the fields but also on the page, in music, on celluloid. A people who produce a distinctive culture earn the right to be thought of as a nation. Colonial rulers would refuse to take seriously the idea that the colony could be a cohesive potentially autonomous nation: the colonized responded by ramping up their cultural production. A good example of this dynamic in recent times comes with the Palestinians. In 1969 Golda Meir famously proclaimed that the Palestinian people did not exist. They responded with an explosive outpouring of literary, cinematic, and artistic production, such that Palestinian culture has become read and exhibited all over the world. However, Zionism itself suggests that cultural production in itself is not enough, for it was based on the idea that without a country of their own, Jewish people would never be respected.

Language and Translation

Indeed, in many respects, she was quite English, and was an excellent example of the fact that we have really everything in common with America nowadays, except, of course, language. (Oscar Wilde, "The Canterville Ghost," 1887)

Just as the world is divided up into nations, so it is divided into different languages. You might argue that nations are in some sense created, whereas languages are "natural." Languages, like nations, however, can be made and transformed, usually for political purposes. The classification of languages certainly has nothing natural about it. The result is that some languages are categorized as the same when they are full of differences (Arabic), whereas other languages are given different names when they are essentially the same (Hindi/Urdu, Dutch/Flemish, Croatian/Serbian). These are politically charged issues – Catalan used to be classified as a dialect of Castilian Spanish, whereas today it is regarded as a separate language, its closest analogue being Occitan, the language of Southern France that was suppressed over the centuries in favor of (Northern) French. Naming languages as distinct entities, with each name designating a single, discrete language, allowed the identification of a language with the idea of a people (in fact in all likelihood similarly fluid in their identity) or a "race," which in turn facilitated the development of the idea of nations. Conversely, having made that identification, the rulers of such a nation would then attempt to destroy any linguistic diversity, as happened in France at the time of the revolution, in the same way that at times nationalists promoted racial or religious homogeneity.

As we have already seen in the discussion of cultural nationalism, for many years, the question of the power relation of the colonial language to colonized languages was a fundamental political question, central to some formulations of anticolonialism. Colonial, or formerly colonized, writers such as the Kenyan Ngũgĩ wa Thiong'o began to write in their native languages: literature was articulated as a form of resistance, of "writing back." Ngũgĩ argued that in using English, the world that he was trying to portray, its very epistemological foundation, was already translated in certain respects into the cultural perspectives of the very colonial culture that he was trying to resist (Ngũgĩ 1981). By contrast, the Nigerian novelist Chinua Achebe contended that English, though the colonizer's language, was effectively now also an African language and one that had become inflected in its new milieu (Achebe 1988). The writer could use English, but should continually subvert it by inflecting it toward local idioms. In making this argument, Achebe was following the lead of James Joyce and other Irish writers, and this in practice is the strategy that most postcolonial writers, from Erna Brodber to Ken Saro-Wiwa, have followed, writing in an English that at the same time has been distinctively transformed into a local idiom. In recent years, the traditional nationalist language debate has been somewhat overtaken by other concerns: for example, English has become the language of preference for Dalit writers in India who want to write in the freedom of a casteless language (Kothari 2013). Elsewhere, the development of a globalized literary market place, dominated by transnational publishing corporations, has meant that English is no longer regarded as a colonial language but operates as the accommodating lingua franca in which all cultures meet. The revival of World Literature has perhaps occurred in part to match this new global condition of commercial publishing.

One corollary of the rise of a World Literature that is predominantly read in English has been the development of an increased interest in the question of translation. More generally, as part of its general interest in cultural diversity, postcolonial studies has been centrally concerned with the differences between languages and issues of translation. In a hierarchical world of economic power and corresponding cultural value, languages exist according to more or less the same scale of significance. Currently, English is the dominant global language, followed by the major European languages, Chinese and Japanese. The rest of the world's six or seven thousand languages in this context are regarded as minor. With the pressures and potential of globalization, more and more people are using or writing in English. However, there is no reason to suppose that the place of English is permanent, for no more than any empire, no language has remained dominant forever (as the very term "lingua franca" suggests). Whereas, traditionally, translation studies was concerned with conceptual or practical issues about translation, working with the basic European paradigm of fidelity or license, in a postcolonial frame the question becomes what are the respective power relations between the languages being translated. How does that affect the translation itself, and the direction and volume of translational activities (e.g., English to Sami, or Amharic to German)? What is the effect of the fact that most translations in the world are made through relay translation (most typically, through a translation of the English translation)? And how far does translation have to take into account Ngũgĩ's argument cited above, a version of the Sapir–Whorf hypothesis, that in a different language you can say different things, and that in certain respects the syntax and vocabulary will express a different worldview? Language, or even the kind of script in which a language is written, can determine the kind of thoughts that you can have, and the conceptual or cultural categories that you will be able to think with. Even particular words, as Walter Benjamin pointed out, that according to the dictionary describe the exact same thing – *brot, pain,* bread – will not only designate different realities of bread (something black and heavy, something long, light, and crusty, something sliced and covered with plastic), but will also have different historical values, significance, and meaning in the local culture. Translation is never impossible – nothing is untranslatable – but translation will always produce transformation, in culture as well as language.

Race, Ethnicity, Identity

One of the main conceptual interventions of postcolonialism was to add, or rather restore, the issue of race to analyses of history, culture, or politics. While race was a ubiquitous reference amongst western commentators up to World War II, the response to its discredited status after 1945 was largely to stop mentioning it altogether. That was easy if you were white: you could just pretend that it had never existed. If you were a person of color, however, not only the history of racialism as a mode of domination – in slavery, in empire – but also the continuing experience of everyday racism created a perspective and situation that was entirely different. While approaching the topic in a very different way from the prewar period, antithetical in fact to its earlier history and contesting its claims, postcolonialism, therefore, emphasizes the importance of race in society and in history. It takes its cue from the UNESCO statement on race published after World War II, which challenged the scientific pretensions of racial theory that had become part of the official ideology of Nazi Germany Italy, and Imperial Japan (UNESCO 1969). Racialism assumed a seamless correlation between biological and cultural characteristics, together with moral and intellectual abilities, but in fact there is no necessary connection between any of these things. The word that UNESCO proposed to put in its place, "ethnicity," contains many of the same associations, and does not deny some degree of physical difference, particularly skin, eye, and hair color. By contrast, however, it emphasizes the cultural aspects of an ethnic identity, such as language, religion, sedentary or nomadic habits, or food. Ethnic identities, however, are no more definitive than those of language: on many occasions they overlap, blur, and run into each other, so that ethnic identity becomes as much a matter of cultural and political choice as anything else, particularly for individuals in western societies. Such questions became particularly important in the late twentieth century as a result of mass emigration and immigration around the world, so that people of different "ethnicities," who had hitherto rarely mixed, found themselves living side by side. One outcome of that, particularly in western countries, was that ethnicities themselves became mixed and the idea of distinctive ethnicities or cultures began to break down. At the same time, the realization that the nation, despite its traditional aspiration to homogeneity, in fact for the most part contains a vast range of different kinds of people, has transformed attitudes toward the idea of the nation itself. There are very few nation-states in the world today that still pursue a single racial, ethnic, or religious identity as some nations did in the nineteenth and early twentieth centuries. For the most part, it is recognized that such totalizing aspirations are unsustainable and will never be realized. For this reason, much political and cultural work in postcolonial states has been to challenge some of the purifying practices of the new state in its self-formation. Before statehood, on the other hand, such political activists would have been doing the very reverse, that is helping to create a common sense of a nation from a colony made up of diverse and different communities. The achievement of nationhood marks the moment when diversity can emerge once more. This suggests that there is an unresolved paradox around the very concept of ethnicity when it moves into political practice: that though its qualities define a people as being a consensual group, the realization of that identity in the form of the state promptly draws out the differences rather than the similarities between them.

In relation to nationalisms and nations, therefore, ethnicity can operate in two ways: to create the nation, and then to challenge its demand for conformism. It can work to give an identity to a "people" who, on the principles of nationalism, demand their own nation and land. From Poles in the Russian Empire to diasporic Jews (who may also have been Poles in the Russian Empire), the cultivation of the sense of a communal identity can work extraordinarily powerfully as a political force. In recent times, the same can be observed among Catalans in Spain or Ghorkas in India: in a postcolonial world of nation-states, ethnicities now work at a political level as the basis of the identity of minorities who feel oppressed in a state made up of a different majority. Whether it be Kurds in Turkey, Iran, and Iraq, Tamils in Sri Lanka, Baluchis in Pakistan, Uyghurs in China, or Chechyns in Russia, ethnic identity operates as a primary form around which agitation for autonomy or independence typically coalesces. In more democratic countries, ethnicity denotes a "minority" identity where the great paradox of democracy – that it enforces the tyrannical rule of the majority – may be mediated by the state with special provisions for ethnic minorities which signal understanding of their particular problems and cultural respect for their specific differences. In Canada, the political formation of "multiculturalism" was developed in order to accommodate the different ethnic groups: English and French-speaking Canadians, and indigenous First Nations. With the advent of mass immigration in Europe many governments followed suit, without understanding that ethnic identity in such situations was much more fluid and mixed than the Canadian model ever envisaged. At its most challenging, therefore, postcolonial theory and related contemporary fiction took the form not of an espousal of multiculturalism as is sometimes assumed, but of its critique, challenging the idea that individuals have a pregiven single ethnic identity, suggesting instead a more

Caribbean structure where such identities are malleable and effectively created by people themselves in response to the demands of their location. Above all, most immigrants will not have a single monolithic ethnic identity, but incorporate shared aspects from different constituencies: a "South Asian" may well not speak any of the languages of the subcontinent, have been brought up France, have parents who though "Indian" came from Trinidad, be a professor of Chinese, enjoy listening to classical music, not be attached definitively to any specific form of sexuality, and dress like an American in jeans and trainers. Sometimes she might feel Indian, at other times Caribbean or French or queer, none of which define her as a person in any definitive way. In fact, everyone, however varied or uniform their backgrounds and interests, takes on different forms of identity at different times of the day, depending on which particular role they are fulfilling (parent, child, executive, legal witness, shopper, cook). Some are more important than others, some are more chosen, and some mandated. Even the most official form of identity, the passport, no longer signifies a definitive identity unless the state issuing that passport will not allow the holder to possess another: in a world of multiple origins, it is not uncommon to meet people who have two or three.

Subalternity

The postcolonial account of identity, therefore, does not emphasize identity as an intrinsic characteristic so much as social and political positioning in particular locations. When a Spaniard flies from Madrid to New York, as soon as the plane touches down on the tarmac at Kennedy Airport he or she is transformed from a first-world European to a third-world "Hispanic." In postcolonial language, the Spaniard has become a "subaltern." What does this mean?

"Subaltern Studies" was the name of a book-series of essays written by historians of India, such as Ranajit Guha, Partha Chatterjee, Dipesh Chakrabarty and others, that began in 1982. The term "subaltern" was taken from the *Prison Notebooks* of the Italian Communist Party leader Antonio Gramsci, where he uses it to describe "subaltern groups" or lower classes, as a complementary term to more classic Marxist categories such as the working class or the peasantry. In adapting it from Gramsci, Guha took the term "subaltern" to mean people of lower rank, and to that degree the term "subaltern" comes very close to James C. Scott's concept of the "subordinated group" (Guha 1982; Scott 1985, 1990). Since then, "subaltern" has come to be used to refer to those who find themselves in a subordinated position within any hierarchical organization or social formation. Scott argued against Gramsci that such people, particularly the peasantry, were in fact much more resistant to dominance and hegemony of their own volition than Gramsci had allowed. The subordinate, in other words, are always insubordinate. For his part, Guha employed the term "subaltern" in order to develop a different position from the then dominant groups of Indian historians, the nationalists and the Marxists. The subaltern studies historians were interested in looking at forms of political activity or insurgency in India that could be classified neither as nationalist anticolonialism nor as working-class activism. The larger suggestion was that nationalist and Marxist accounts of Indian history had overlooked the activities of a whole range of people who did not fall within these categories, particularly the peasantry, whose main conflict was a feudal one with Indian landowners rather than with the British, or whose activities and resistances involved practices such as religion that were not taken seriously by secular historians. Guha's ideas were subsequently employed and extended by South American historians for their own particular situations (Rodriguez 2001). Subaltern studies, therefore, was not so much a critique of colonialism as a critique of the writing of history itself, a question that has always been at the heart of postcolonial studies, which has sought to develop ways in which the world's history might be written outside the traditional perspective and framework of the expansion of Europe (Chakrabarty 2000; Young 2004). Subsequently, the subaltern studies group itself divided between those who continued to espouse a more traditional form of social history and those who, influenced by the ideas of postcolonial theory, moved into a "culturalist" mode.

Three years after subaltern studies had begun, the Indian cultural critic Gayatri Chakravorty Spivak made a significant intervention in which she pointed to the missing category of gender among the subaltern studies historians: women were a further group who had predictably been given no attention by male historians, but whose position with respect to nationalist or Marxist agendas was similar to that of subalterns generally. Their agenda was as much oriented toward their own liberation from patriarchy as national liberation. In making this intervention, Spivak also shifted the concept of the subaltern away from Gramsci's emphasis on the group to that of the individual, at which point the idea of the subaltern woman became that of woman as subaltern. In her celebrated essay, "Can the Subaltern Speak?," Spivak took the case of an Indian widow who was expected, according to the Hindu tradition of *sati*, to throw herself alive on the funeral pyre of her husband (Spivak 1988). The British colonial administrators sought to stop this practice, but they were resisted by (male) Hindu nationalists who argued that the British were trying to destroy their sacred Hindu heritage. In this battle of wills between two groups of males drawing on their own discourses of human rights and religious tradition, respectively, Spivak pointed out that there was no space for the woman herself to speak and make an intervention – whatever she chose to do, the meaning of her action had been already appropriated by the men. A similar situation obtains today in traditional societies when women who assert themselves against patriarchal customs are immediately branded as simply mimicking western ideology. Any form of feminism can be easily dismissed as just being an anti-religious western idea, even though the West has historically certainly had no monopoly on women's self-assertion against patriarchy, or indeed men's – for example, the nineteenth-century Egyptian Qasim Amin.

The concept of the subaltern, whether speaking or not, has become hugely influential within postcolonial studies: it is broad enough to encompass a whole range of situations of subalternity globally, from migrant women workers cleaning toilets at academic conferences in Boston to Indian workers tapping rubber on plantations in Malaysia. Its advantage is precisely that since it describes a structural power relation, it can encompass a far wider variety of positions than the classic category of the proletariat or working class, which requires, in the first instance, an industrial economy. Its disadvantage is that, as its adoption by the subaltern studies historians suggests, "subaltern" is an academic word used to describe other people in a certain situation, not a word with which they would describe themselves. Most people would in any case depict themselves in terms of their own particular individuality or group, rather than through a general concept. On the other hand, "worker" or "working class" became and remains a form of self-identification for many. The subaltern has never achieved this kind of use, and remains more comparable to the analytical use of "the proletariat," a term with which few workers self-identified. The term "subaltern" therefore can be useful in pointing to the sharing of structurally similar power positions across a wide range of different situations. Its drawback is that the very use of the term is objectifying, and to that degree the word itself constructs and repeats the same disparate power relation which it seeks to highlight.

Such objectification will always be present when the term "subaltern" is used in its original form, either for political analysis, as in Gramsci, or for historical analysis, as in the work of the subaltern studies historians. Gramsci's own writings on subaltern classes in the *Prison Notebooks* are in fact comparatively brief. More relevant in many ways to the postcolonial is his focus on the *emarginati*, marginalized people. In his biography of Gramsci, Dante Germino has shown how Gramsci's own position as a *gobbo*, a hunchback, led him to focus on all the groups in society who occupied positions of social and political marginalization (Forgacs 2014; Germino 1990). While politics was played out by rival power groups at the center, Gramsci also paid consistent attention to those who never had access to this domain, but lived marginal lives at the peripheries of society. This perspective – identifying with the marginalized – represents the radical focus of his politics, and better characterizes the focus of his political sympathies that go beyond the mainstream categories of class. Gramsci's stress on those who live on the fringes of the social order can be compared to the French philosopher Jacques Rancière's emphasis on the poor, on the count of those who do not count (Rancière 2004). A preoccupation with the emarginated, with outcast individuals or subordinated social groups, comes closest to the politics of postcolonialism, which is most concerned with those who, within the structures of power that operate within and between societies, live out their lives at the fringes and peripheries of the world. The Dalits in India live a life of permanent exclusion from the moment of birth. Elsewhere, millions of people live permanently stateless within states that they have never left because of the shifting identities of states, citizenship legislation, and wars: the Bidoon (literally, the "Without") in the Gulf States, Muslim Rohingyas from Myanmar in Bangladesh, Nubians in Kenya, Dalits in Nepal.[1] The speech of the subordinated is mute not because they are not speaking but because their voices remain unheard because no one thinks of listening to them. Such concerns in turn link back to the subaltern studies historians, whose own early political sympathies were widely identified with the Naxalites, the "hungry tide" of radical Maoists who operate in the so-called "red corridor" in India, controlling large swathes of the countryside through twelve states, from West Bengal down through the Eastern states further south (Chakravarti 2008).

Indigeneity

Many, perhaps the majority, of people on earth live in, or relatively near, the place in which they were born. But not everyone, on that basis, is called a native, or an aboriginal, or an indigenous person. While "aboriginal" in English usually functions as a proper name that designates the indigenous people of Australia (though it is also sometimes invoked elsewhere), "indigenous" is used very widely around the world. What makes a person or a people "indigenous?" Simply put, native to indigenous is similar to race to ethnicity: the first word of each pairing designates the old term that is no longer used (though you will still find the adjectival form of native, as in "a native Londoner" or "native speaker"), the second the modern acceptable alternative. The aura of "native" still circulates around "indigenous," evoking a people who are seen as being in some sense outside modernity. This is not, of course, how it will probably seem to them (Clifford 2013). Who qualifies as indigenous is complicated by the fact that there is no generally acceptable definition of the term (Coates 2004: 1–2). The UN Declaration of the Rights of Indigenous Peoples now affirms many rights for indigenous peoples but never once defines who they are or who qualifies as indigenous to hold these rights. The problem is generally solved in a liberal way so that anyone who considers themselves indigenous qualifies as indigenous, but at the same time, in practice the term is used to designate relatively small groups of culturally cohesive people who are held to have an ancestral relation to the land in which they live but over which they may have no formal legal rights according to the precepts of modern law. We have already discussed (in chapter 3) how colonizers brought with them a legal system which by its own criteria of proof and evidence disqualified the entitlement of indigenous inhabitants to their own lands, although indigenous people made every attempt to assert their rights (Belmessous 2014). We have also considered the situation of indigenous peoples in settler postcolonies in the previous chapter: the concept of indigenous peoples is particularly apparent in a colonial situation such as the United States or Canada, where the clash of indigene and settler has historically been deepest and most dramatic, or at least perceived as such thanks to its high profiling in twentieth-century Hollywood movies symptomatically called "Westerns."

The status of indigenous peoples in former colonies remains one of the most pressing "postcolonial" political issues. In the twenty-first century, in Australia, Aotearoa/New Zealand, and the Americas, many continue to be separated from majority populations descended from the settler elites. This is the case, for example, in Bolivia, which has the highest proportion of indigenous peoples in South America (although in 2005, Bolivia elected its first president of indigenous origin, Evo Morales), and in Mexico, where the country is predominantly of mixed ethnicity (*mestizo*), but where groups such as the Zapatistas in Chiapas in the Southeast of the country identify as indigenous and have developed effective political campaigns, being the first to use social media. They correlate their marginal position with an anti-globalization campaign in what might be termed a politics of indigenous socialism, allying with *campesinos* (small-scale farmers) and campaigners for landless people. Indigenous politics differs from mainstream socialism not only in its rural focus, but also in the importance of environmentalism: under Morales, Bolivia has legislated the Ley de Derechos de la Madre Tierra (the Law of the Rights of Mother Earth), which invests nature with the same rights as human beings, drawing on indigenous beliefs that nature and the land are sacred, the *Pachamama* on which humanity depends. As the law states, "Mother Earth is a living dynamic system made up of the undivided community of all living beings, who are all interconnected, interdependent, and complementary, sharing a common destiny."[2] The connections between the politics of indigenism and environmentalism join seamlessly as part of the campaigns for indigenous rights against land exploitation and appropriation, mineral and gas extraction, on traditional tribal lands. Indigenous people show the way in embodying a way of life that is ecologically much more efficient and responsive to the ecosystem than that of the world's urban populations. Indigenous forms of knowledge offer a different relation to the natural world. Instead of seeking to triumph over nature, as western reason and technology have done since the eighteenth century, indigenous knowledge sees human beings as part of a natural process in all its dimensions, establishing over generations a relation of care between themselves and their natural environment, along with skills of survival developed in reciprocal relation to the natural world. Although it would be foolish to assume that they remain uncontaminated and entirely separate from the pressures of the world around them, contrast, in general, the lifestyle of Amazonian Indians with the resource extractors destroying the Amazon rain forests; compare the lives of aboriginal peoples in Australia with those evacuating the earth outside Perth in order to send minerals and metals to China so that it can build yet more uninhabited ghost cities for wealthy Chinese to invest in.

However, there are many countries, sometimes also former colonies but without recent settler populations, where indigenous peoples, such as the so-called tribals or *adivasi* of India, live in a state of disadvantage and exploitation. The difference is that in settler colonies the relatively recent arrival of settlers of a different ethnicity from far away makes their appropriation of the land and the country rather different, at a political level, from those many countries around the world where indigenous peoples continue to live as part of a historically evolved society. The result is that indigenous peoples in non-settler colonies are often in the worst situation of all: they cannot count on any liberal colonial guilt in the main population.

The politics of the postcolonial, which comprises the tradition of the oppressed, is identified with people who are socially and politically marginalized in their everyday existence, and is therefore particularly preoccupied with the situation of indigenous peoples, with peoples of the "fourth world" wherever they may live, whether it be in the Middle East (the Maʿdān), North Africa (the Berber), Southern Africa (the San), South Asia (*Adivasi*, the Naga), East Asia (the Thao, Kavalan, and Truku among others in Taiwan, the Ainu in Japan), the Circumpolar North, or Arctic (the Sami). There is a further link between postcolonial and indigenous politics: indigenous activism in relation to aboriginal rights developed in the context of colonial liberation movements, along with the human and civil rights campaigns of the 1960s. National and local indigenous movements then began to be globalized, beginning in 1975 with the establishment of the World Council of Indigenous Peoples, and the emergence of the Inuit Circumpolar Council which brought together Inuit peoples from Canada, the United States, Russia, and Greenland. As a result of this new globalized activism, in 2007 in a landmark move, the United Nations adopted the UN Declaration of the Rights of Indigenous Peoples: the former settler colonies of Australia, Canada, New Zealand, and the United States all voted against it.

Nomadism

The question of indigenous people and the particular kind of life which they may lead correlates closely to that of "nomadism." Many indigenous peoples are, or were until very recently, nomadic; nomads, such as the Bedouin in the Middle East, cattle farmers in Gujarat, and the Masai in East Africa, are often pastoralists grazing their animals and who move across the landscape according to the season, or hunters, such as the Inuit in North America. Indigenous peoples live, or formerly lived, at radical odds with the western social norm of a stable, settled, sedentary life: their customs are antithetical to those of the settler. We think of life today in terms of being "settled," or in colonial history of "settlers." Yet, for much of their history, most human beings have been nomadic. The shift to a sedentary lifestyle ("sedentarization") started with the shift to crop farming, and has continued over the last two centuries as an effect of industrialization and the ever-increasing control of the state on its population. The nomadic groups that have survived have typically been those who live in less fertile areas that cannot support crop farming but produce instead seasonal produce in different areas of a region. Pastoral nomadism remains the most common traditional form, along with "peri-patetic" nomadism – that is, those who move habitually among sedentary populations, such as gypsies, tinkers, *hijra*, musicians, and dancers.

The French philosopher Gilles Deleuze and psychiatrist Félix Guattari have developed the idea of the nomad as a figure for the person who in modern times most successfully resists the controlling power of the state (Deleuze and Guattari 1988: 380). Modern states, whether in Europe, the Middle East, or Asia, do not like nomadic peoples, people of no fixed abode who cannot be initiated into the controlling processes by which the state's citizens are registered, identified, educated, medicalized, taxed, and organized in many other ways from birth to death. One of the primary pressures of the nation-state in the past two hundred years has been to stop people from moving, to contain them within prescribed boundaries into a settled, controllable condition. The fate of Romanies (gypsies, Roma) and travelers within Europe, or Bedouin in the Middle East, has been to live under a continuous pressure to urbanize and conform to the static requirements of citizenship whereby each person is located with a specific name, number, and locatable place of permanent residence. Nevertheless, their elusive habits, mobility, and lines of flight involve forms of lateral, transnational resistance that continue to offer alternative possibilities to any top-down model of power and resistance.

Migration

> One of the special features of imperialism … is the decline in emigration from imperialist countries and the increase in immigration into these countries from the more backward countries where lower wages are paid. (Lenin 1917: 127)

Although nomadism, as Deleuze and Guattari argued, can represent a powerful form of opposition to the control of the state, in the thirteenth century one nomadic group, the Mongols under Genghis Khan, created the largest land empire in history. The Mongols offer a clear example of the connection between nomadic societies and a phenomenon central to empire and the postcolonial world: migration.[3] If the history of the world has been a history of empires, from a more human point of view and from an even longer perspective it has also been a history of migrations. People have been moving ever since the first humans began to migrate from Africa sixty thousand years ago. It is only in the last ten thousand years, with the development of agriculture, that people have started to settle and stay still. But as the history of empires itself shows, some people have always been on the move and that movement has been one of the primary forces driving political, social, and ecological change – whether it be the migrations of Germanic peoples in Europe from the fourth to sixth centuries, the Mongol and Turkic migrations across Asia from the sixth to the thirteenth centuries, the European and (forced) African migration to the Americas from the sixteenth to the nineteenth centuries, or the migrations of Africans and Asians to Europe and North America in the twentieth and twenty-first centuries. Empires and settler colonies have precipitated many other forced migrations in addition to those of slavery and indentured laborers: from the Scots highlanders in the eighteenth century, to the Irish and Native Americans in the nineteenth century, to the Armenians from the Ottoman Empire, or Palestinians from Palestine, in the twentieth century.

Postcolonialism is concerned with issues that result from many different types of migration: from the formations of empires in earlier centuries to settlers in modern times to migrant workers and illegal migrants in the present. Like contemporary illegal migrants, early settlers such as the Pilgrim Fathers endured punishing physical challenges. The only real difference between settlers of earlier centuries and illegal migrants today is their legality: in a world of nation-states and strict governmental surveillance of populations, agency is refused the migrant and unauthorized migration is declared illegal by the receiving state. While exceptions are, in decreasing numbers, made for those who have fled war or famine, states today are more and more reluctant to accept refugees and asylum seekers in a world in which there are over fifty million refugees, asylum seekers, and internally displaced persons.[4] At the same time, in practice many states do admit the numerous migrants who get caught up in the webs of human trafficking for sexual and other forms of contemporary slavery (Bales 2012).

Today's illegal migrants, the so-called economic migrants, such as those who risk, and often encounter, death by crossing the Sahara and taking small fragile boats from North Africa to Europe, are not inherently any different from European migrants who fled poverty, starvation, or persecution in Europe for Africa or the Americas or Australasia in earlier centuries. The only difference lies in the changed attitude toward migration by the state and by the receiving population (no matter that many of them may have been migrants themselves, or come from migrant families). The dramatic transformation that has taken place with respect to immigration is powerfully evoked in Joseph Conrad's story "Amy Foster," published in 1901 in the world of the Bartholomew atlas described in chapter 1 (Conrad 1903). The novella relates the tale of Yanko, a Polish migrant who is on his way to America when his boat is shipwrecked on the Kent coast in England. He alone survives, only to find himself in an unknown country speaking an incomprehensible tongue. At first the inhabitants are hostile, but they take him in and in time, despite the oddities of his foreignness, he is more or less accepted and even marries a local girl. The story has a traumatic ending, but what is striking from the perspective of migration today is its dramatically different and stark indication of the inhumanity of our own era: despite the initial hostility of the villagers toward Yanko, no one ever thinks of calling a policeman, no one ever asks for his papers or passport. He is not sent to a detention center for illegal migrants and incarcerated indefinitely. The bureaucratic power of the state controlling its citizens' lives down to every last intimate detail is extraordinarily, wonderfully absent (Keenan 2014). "Amy Foster" unwittingly points to our radical loss of freedom, to say nothing of humanity, in the contemporary epoch. The system of nation-states means that human freedom is restricted and controlled with passports, visas, entry permits, borders, walls, security fences, electronic surveillance systems, and detention centers in a way that would have been unimaginable just a hundred years ago. For the Kent villagers, the "crime" of illegal migration simply did not exist, which is very far from the situation today. Today the population of Kent sits on the opposite side of the English Channel to ever-blossoming camps of refugees around Calais, of which the Sangatte camp was the most famous. No sooner is one closed than another appears: these camps are created by the migrants as they prepare to smuggle themselves into England through the Channel Tunnel. Once they arrive in England, of course, they may be put in a real camp, or, in official parlance, an "immigration removal center."[5] In that context, Georgio Agamben's argument that the camp is the "nomos," or the order of the modern, makes perfect sense (Agamben 1995, 1998b). Despite the horror of Nazi concentration camps, the camp has become a major instrument of the contemporary governmentality of the state: for refugees, asylum seekers, illegal migrants of all kinds, for all those who have fled or challenged the order of things in the postcolonial world of nation-states. Of the many camps and detention centers for illegal migrants that now exist in and outside first-world countries, the most inhuman must be Australia's notorious, chillingly named, "Pacific Solution." Illegal migrants caught trying to enter Australia by sea are not allowed to land on Australian territory, but are exported instead to extra-territorial camps elsewhere around the Pacific, some of them on tiny islands such as Nauru, a country of just 21 square kilometers in the South Pacific. For the people of "the lucky country," with a population density only a little higher than Mongolia (2.6 people per square kilometer), out of sight is truly out of mind. The Australian aboriginal community must be wishing that this policy had been in force in 1788 when the British first arrived.

Strict controls on migration constitute a defensive response by nation-states to a new nomadism in the later twentieth and twenty-first centuries, where millions of migrant workers, refugees, and asylum seekers – the "undesirables" of the world (Agier 2011) – move around the planet in response to civil strife, political instability, economic inequality, and the demands of capital (Harding 2012). One effect of globalization is that, whether illegally or legally but temporarily, workers are moving to the sites where their skills are required. Like globalization itself, this operates hierarchically: at the professional level, multinational companies or international organizations deliberately move their executives from country to country as part of their career path, much in the manner of colonial administrators a century ago, while at the other end of the social scale, the migrant workers who travel across the globe, legally or illegally, also in search of a better standard of living, are propelled to do so only because they have been born into a situation where the local standards, and earnings, are so abysmal. Both groups are equally the subjects of global capitalism, undoing national boundaries for its immediate and long-term interests.

Migration flows around the world are the mark of global postcoloniality, as the world's "surplus humanity" flees from violence, civil war, and poverty to places where they believe, in part as a result of the ubiquitous presence of the international media system, that they will have a better life (Davis 2006). The flows of Pakistanis and Sri Lankans trying to get to Australia; Pakistanis, Afghans, and Kurds to London; Maghrebian and sub-Saharan Africans to Italy, France, and Spain; Mexicans to the United States – all these flows bizarrely mirror the nineteenth-century outflow of millions of people from Europe to the Americas, Africa, and Australasia. The risks that modern illegal migrants take – in airless container trucks, walking across the Sahara, sailing in flimsy crowded boats to Christmas Island or Lampedusa – show that they feel they have nothing to lose except their lives: the risks they take show how desperate they are. As they move across borders, they discard their papers, if they had any, to become stateless. If they finally establish themselves, they will send money back to their home country, which will sustain itself on such remittances. Despite their much-heralded rise as global economies, the countries that receive the largest amounts in remittances from their workers who have had to leave and seek work abroad are India and China.[6]

Such movements of migration or displacement are not only transnational, but also take place within the nation. Walk into a railway station in China and you will see groups of workers of all ages and regional ethnicities in rough clothes, sitting on the floor with their bundles of bedding beside them. They are on the move, seeking work. Walk into the railway station in Milan, and you will find it crammed with migrants from the Middle East and Africa, some of them women who have just given birth, who have arrived by boat in Lampedusa and been sent North to fend for themselves. Walk south from Ras Beirut into the Shatila refugee camp and you will find its narrow, constricted spaces, already full to bursting with Palestinian refugees who have been there for decades, teeming with newly arrived fugitives from Iraq and Syria. These are the realities of our postcolonial, globalized, oblivious world.

Notes

1   http://www.unhcr.org/pages/49c3646c155.html.
2   http://www.therightsofnature.org/bolivia-law-of-mother-earth.

3 Deleuze and Guattari claim a fundamental distinction between the nomad and the migrant, but this is made on the assumption that the migrant simply relocates from one place to another. If this was ever true, it is certainly less so today.

4 http://www.unhcr.org/53a155bc6.html.

5 https://www.gov.uk/immigration-removal-centre/overview.

6 http://www.econ.worldbank.org/WBSITE/EXTERNAL/EXTDEC/ EXTDECPROSPECTS/0,,contentMDK:22759429~pagePK:64165401~piPK: 64165026~theSitePK:476883,00.html#Remittances.

References

Aaronsohn, Ran (1996), "Settlement in Eretz Israel – A Colonialist Enterprise? 'Critical' Scholarship and Historical Geography." *Israel Studies* 1: 2, 214–229.

Achebe, Chinua (1988), *Hopes and Impediments: Selected Essays 1965–1987*. London: Heinemann.

Adiga, Aravind (2008), *The White Tiger*. New York: Free Press.

Agamben, Giorgio (1995), "We Refugees." *Symposium*, 49: 2, 114–119.

Agamben, Giorgio (1998a), "Beyond Human Rights." *Social Engineering* 15: 90–95.

Agamben, Giorgio (1998b), *Homo Sacer: Sovereign Power and Bare Life*, trans. Daniel Heller-Roazen. Stanford: Stanford University Press.

Agier, Michel (2011), *Managing the Undesirables: Refugee Camps and Humanitarian Government*. Cambridge: Polity.

Allen, Robert C. (2011), *Global Economic History: A Very Short Introduction*. Oxford: Oxford University Press.

Alvarez, Alex (2014), *Native America and the Question of Genocide*. Lanham, MD: Rowman and Littlefield.

Anderson, Benedict (1983), *Imaginary Communities: Reflections on the Origins and Spread of Nationalism*. London: Verso.

Anidjar, Gil (2002), *"Our Place in al-Andalus": Kabbalah, Philosophy, Literature in Arab Jewish Letters*. Stanford: Stanford University Press.

Arendt, Hannah (1958) [1951], *The Origins of Totalitarianism*, 2nd ed. Cleveland: Meridian Books.

Armitage, David (2007), *The Declaration of Independence: A Global History.* Boston: Harvard University Press.

Asad, Talal (2003), *Formations of the Secular: Christianity, Islam and Modernity.* Stanford: Stanford University Press.

Badie, Bertrand and Vidal, Dominique, eds. (2014), *Nouvelles guerres: L'état du monde 2015.* Paris: La Découverte.

Bahadur, Gaiutra (2013), *Coolie Woman: The Odyssey of Indenture.* London: Hurst.

Bailyn, Bernard (2013), *The Barbarous Years: The Peopling of British North America – the Conflict of Civilizations, 1600–1675.* New York: Vintage.

Bakhtin, M. M. (1968), *Rabelais and His World,* trans. Hélène Iwolsky. Cambridge, MA: MIT Press.

Bales, Kevin (2012), *Disposable People: New Slavery in the Global Economy,* rev. ed. Berkeley: University of California Press.

Barnard, F. M. (2003), *Herder on Nationality, Humanity, and History.* Montreal: McGill-Queen's University Press.

Barr, James (2012), *A Line in the Sand: Britain, France, and the Struggle that Shaped the Middle East.* New York: Simon and Schuster.

Bartholomew, J. G. (1902), *The Century Atlas of the World.* London: John Walker.

Bauman, Zygmunt (2004), *Wasted Lives: Modernity and Its Outcasts.* Cambridge: Polity.

Bayart, Jean-François (1993) [1989], *The State in Africa: The Politics of the Belly,* trans. Mary Harper, Christopher Harison, and Elizabeth Harison. London: Longman.

Bayly, C. A. (1996), *Empire and Information: Intelligence Gathering and Social Communication in India, 1780–1870.* Cambridge: Cambridge University Press.

Bayly, Christopher and Harper, Tim (2005), *Forgotten Armies: Britain's Asian Empire and War with Japan.* London: Penguin.

Bell, Duncan (2009), *The Idea of Greater Britain: Empire and the Future of World Order, 1860–1900.* Princeton: Princeton University Press.

Belmessous, Saliha, ed. (2014), *Native Claims: Indigenous Law against Empire, 1500–1920.* Oxford: Oxford University Press.

Benjamin, Walter (2003), "On the Concept of History," in *Selected Writings 1938–1940* vol. 4, ed. Howard Eiland and Michael W. Jennings. Cambridge, MA: Harvard University Press, 389–400.

Benton, Lauren (2010), *A Search for Sovereignty: Law and Geography in European Empires, 1400–1900.* Cambridge: Cambridge University Press.

Betts, Raymond (2004), *Decolonization.* London: Routlege.

Bhabha, Homi K. (1994), *The Location of Culture*. London: Routledge

Bingham, Tom (2010), *The Rule of Law*. London: Allen Lane.

Blackburn, Robin (1988), *The Overthrow of Colonial Slavery, 1776–1848*. London: Verso.

Borges, Jorge Luis (1999), "John Wilkins' Analytical Language," in *Selected Non-Fictions*, ed. Eliot Weinberger. New York: Penguin, 229–232.

Bourdieu, Pierre (1984), *Distinction: A Social Critique of the Judgement of Taste*, trans. Richard Nice. London: Routledge.

Bragança, Aquino de and Wallerstein, Immanuel, eds. (1982), *The African Liberation Reader*. 3 vols. London: Zed Books.

Brooks, Rosa Ehrenreich (2003), "The New Imperialism: Violence, Norms, and the 'Rule of Law.'" *Michigan Law Review* 101: 7, 2275–2340.

Buck-Morss, Susan (2009), *Hegel, Haiti and Universal History*. Pittsburgh: Pittsburgh University Press.

Bukharin, Nikolai (1972) [1924], *Imperialism and the Accumulation of Capital*. New York: Monthly Review Press.

Bulwer, John (1654), *A View of the People of the Whole World*. London: Hunt.

Burbank, Jane and Cooper, Frederick (2010), *Empires in World History: Power and the Politics of Difference*. Princeton: Princeton University Press.

Burleigh, Michael and Wippermann, Wolfgang (1991), *The Racial State: Germany 1933–1945*. Cambridge: Cambridge University Press.

Cabral, Amilcar (1973), *Return to the Source: Selected Speeches by Amilcar Cabral*. New York: Monthly Review Press with Africa Information Service.

Cain, P. J. and Hopkins, A. G. (1993a), *British Imperialism: Innovation and Expansion, 1688–1914*. London: Longman.

Cain, P. J. and Hopkins, A. G. (1993b), *British Imperialism: Crisis and Deconstruction, 1914–1990*. London: Longman.

Cannadine, David (2001), *Ornamentalism: How the British Saw Their Empire*. London: Allen Lane.

Carpentier, Alejo (2001) [1953], *The Lost Steps*, trans. Harriet de Onís. Minneapolis: University of Minnesota Press.

Casanova, Pascale (2004) [1999], *The World Republic of Letters*, trans. M. B. DeBevoise. Cambridge, MA: Harvard University Press.

Cassano, Franco (2011), *Southern Thought, and Other Essays on the Mediterranean*, trans. Norma Bouchard and Valerio Ferme. New York: Fordham University Press.

Césaire, Aimé (1950), *Discours sur le colonialisme*. Paris: Réclame.

Césaire, Aimé (1972), *Discourse on Colonialism*, trans. Joan Pinkham. New York: Monthly Review Press.

Chakrabarty, Dipesh (2000), *Provincializing Europe: Postcolonial Thought and Historical Difference*. Princeton: Princeton University Press.

Chakravarti, Sudeep (2008), *Red Sun: Travel in Naxalite Country*. New Delhi: Viking.

Chamayou, Grégoire (2013), *Théorie du drone*. Paris: La Fabrique editions.

Chamberlain, M. E. (1999), *Decolonization: The Fall of the European Empires*. Oxford: Wiley-Blackwell.

Chandra, Sudhir (2008), *Enslaved Daughters: Colonialism, Law and Women's Rights*. Delhi: Oxford University Press.

Chatterjee, Nandini (n.d.), "Law and the British Empire," http://www.privycouncilpapers.org/contexts/law-and-british-empire/.

Chatterjee, Partha (1986), *Nationalist Thought and the Colonial World: A Derivative Discourse*. London: Zed Books.

Chatterjee, Partha (1993), *The Nation and Its Fragments: Colonial and Postcolonial Histories*. Princeton: Princeton University Press.

Chaudhuri, Nupur and Strobel, Margaret (1992), *Western Women and Imperialism: Complicity and Resistance*. Bloomington: Indiana University Press.

Clifford, James (2013), *Returns: Becoming Indigenous in the Twenty-First Century*. Cambridge, MA: Harvard University Press.

Coates, Ken S. (2004), *A Global History of Indigenous Peoples: Struggle and Survival*. Basingstoke: Palgrave Macmillan.

Conrad, Joseph (1902) [1899], "Heart of Darkness," in *Youth: A Narrative, and Two Other Stories*. London: William Blackwood.

Conrad, Joseph (1903) [1901], "Amy Foster," in *Typhoon and Other Stories*. London: William Heinemann.

Coyle, Diane (2014), *GDP: A Brief but Affectionate History*. Princeton: Princeton University Press.

Crosby, Alfred W. (2003), *The Columbian Exchange: Biological and Cultural Consequences of 1492*, 2nd ed. New York: Praeger.

Crosby, Alfred W. (2004), *Ecological Imperialism. The Biological Expansion of Europe 900–1900*, 2nd ed. Cambridge: Cambridge University Press.

Dabashi, Hamid (2012), *The Arab Spring: The End of Postcolonialism*. London: Zed Books.

Damrosch, David (2003), *What is World Literature?* Princeton: Princeton University Press.

Darwin, John (2013), *Unfinished Empire: The Global Expansion of Britain*. London: Penguin.

Davis, Lance E. and Huttenback, Robert A. (1986), *Mammon and the Pursuit of Empire: The Political Economy of British Imperialism, 1860–1912*. Cambridge: Cambridge University Press.

Davis, Mike (2006), *Planet of Slums*. London: Verso.

de Bolla, Peter (2014), *The Architecture of Concepts: The Historical Formation of Human Rights*. New York: Fordham University Press.

Deleuze, Gilles and Guattari, Félix (1988) [1980], *A Thousand Plateaus: Capitalism and Schizophrenia*, vol. 2, trans. Brian Massumi. London: Athlone.

Delrio, Walter, Lenton, Diana, Musante, Marcelo, Nagy, Mariano, Papazian, Alexis, and Pérez, Pilar (2010), "Discussing Indigenous Genocide in Argentina: Past, Present, and Consequences of Argentinean State Policies Toward Native Peoples." *Genocide Studies and Prevention* 5: 2, 138–159.

Desai, Kiran (2006), *The Inheritance of Loss*. London: Hamish Hamilton.

de Saint-Exupéry, Antoine (1944) [1943], *The Little Prince*, trans. Katherine Woods. London: Heinemann.

Devji, Faisal (2013), *Muslim Zion: Pakistan as a Political Idea*. London: Hurst.

Dubois, Laurent (2004), *A Colony of Citizens: Revolution and Slave Emancipation in the French Caribbean, 1787–1804*. Chapel Hill: University of North Carolina Press.

Fanon, Frantz (1965) [1959], *A Dying Colonialism*, trans. Haakon Chevalier. New York: Grove Press.

Fanon, Frantz (1966) [1961], *The Wretched of the Earth*, trans. Constance Farrington. New York: Grove Press.

Fanon, Frantz (1986) [1952], *Black Skin, White Masks*, trans. Charles Lam Markmann. London: Pluto Press.

Ferguson, Niall (2002), *Empire: How Britain Made the Modern World*. London: Allen Lane.

Fieldhouse, D. K. (1982), *The Colonial Empires: A Comparative Survey from the Eighteenth Century*. London: Macmillan.

Forgacs, David (2014), *Italy's Margins: Social Exclusion and Nation Formation since 1861*. Cambridge: Cambridge University Press.

Foucault, Michel (2003), *Society Must Be Defended: Lectures at the Collège de France, 1975–76*, trans. David Macey. New York: Picador.

Gallagher, John and Robinson, Ronald (1953), "The Imperialism of Free Trade," *Economic History Review* n.s. 6: 1, 1–15.

Gandhi, M. K. (1997), *Hind Swaraj, and Other Writings*, ed. Anthony J. Parel. Cambridge: Cambridge University Press.

Germino, Dante (1990), *Antonio Gramsci: Architect of a New Politics*. Baton Rouge: Louisiana State University Press.

Gilroy, Paul (1993), *The Black Atlantic: Modernity and Double Consciousness*. London: Verso.

Gilroy, Paul (2010), "Declaration of Rights," in *Darker Than Blue: On the Moral Economies of Black Atlantic Culture*. Cambridge, MA: Harvard University Press, 55–119.

Gilroy, Paul (2013), "Postcolonialism and Cosmopolitanism: Towards a Worldly Understanding of Fascism and Europe's Colonial Crimes," in Rosi Braidotti, Patrick Hanafin, and Bolette B. Blaagaard, eds., *After Cosmopolitanism*. London: Routledge, 111–131.

Ginsburg, Tom (2011), "In Defense of Imperialism? The Rule of Law and the State Building Project," in James Fleming, ed., *Getting to the Rule of Law: Nomos L*. New York: New York University Press, 224–240.

Glyn, Andrew (2006), *Capitalism Unleashed: Finance, Globalization and Welfare*. Oxford: Oxford University Press.

Goody, Jack (2006), *The Theft of History*. Cambridge: Cambridge University Press.

Goody, Jack (2012), *Metals, Culture and Capitalism: An Essay on the Origins of the Modern World*. Cambridge: Cambridge University Press.

Greene, Jack P., ed. (2009), *Exclusionary Empire: English Liberty Overseas, 1600–1900*. Cambridge: Cambridge University Press.

Guha, Ranajit (1982), "Preface," *Subaltern Studies I: Writings on South Asian History and Society*. Delhi: Oxford University Press, vii–viii.

Guha, Ranajit (1997), *Dominance without Hegemony: History and Power in Colonial India*. Cambridge, MA: Harvard University Press.

Guha, Ranajit and Spivak, Gayatri Chakravorty, eds. (1988), *Selected Subaltern Studies*. New York: Oxford University Press.

Hansen, Peo and Jonsson, Stefan (2013), *Eurafrica: An Untold History*. London: Bloomsbury.

Harding, Jeremy (2012), *Border Vigils: Keeping Migrants Out of the Rich World*. London: Verso.

Hardt, Michael and Negri, Antonio (2000), *Empire*. Cambridge, MA: Harvard University Press.

Harvey, David (2005), *A Brief History of Neoliberalism*. Oxford: Oxford University Press.

Heartfield, James (2011), *The Aborigines' Protection Society: Humanitarian Imperialism in Australia, New Zealand, Fiji, Canada, South Africa, and the Congo, 1837–1909*. London: Hurst.

Hill, Christopher (1972), *The World Turned Upside Down: Radical Ideas during the English Revolution*. New York: Viking.

Hippler, Thomas (2013), *Bombing the People: Giulio Douhet and the Foundations of Air-Power Strategy, 1884–1939*. Cambridge: Cambridge University Press.

Hobsbawm, Eric (1985), *The Age of Capital: 1848–1875*. London: Weidenfeld and Nicolson.

Hobsbawm, Eric (1987), *The Age of Empire: 1875–1914*. London, Weidenfeld and Nicolson.

Hobsbawm, Eric (1990), *Nations and Nationalism Since 1870: Programme, Myth, Reality*. Cambridge: Cambridge University Press.

Hobsbawm, Eric and Ranger, Terence, eds. (1983), *The Invention of Tradition*. Cambridge: Cambridge University Press.

Hobson, J. A. (1902), *Imperialism: A Study*. London: James Nisbet.

Hodge, Joseph Morgan (2007), *Triumph of the Expert: Agrarian Doctrines of Development and the Legacies of British Colonialism*. Athens: Ohio University Press.

Howe, Stephen (2002), *Empire: A Very Short Introduction*. Oxford: Oxford University Press.

Huzzey, Richard (2012), *Freedom Burning: Anti-Slavery and Empire in Victorian Britain*. Ithaca: Cornell University Press.

James, C. L. R. (2001) [1938], *The Black Jacobins: Toussaint L'ouverture and the San Domingo Revolution*. London: Penguin.

Jayawardena, Kumari (1995), *The White Woman's Other Burden: Western Women and South Asia During British Rule*. London: Routledge.

Jebb, Richard (1905), *Studies in Colonial Nationalism*. London: Edward Arnold.

Kaldor, Mary (1999), *New and Old Wars: Organized Violence in a Global Era*. Stanford: Stanford University Press.

Keen, David (2012), *Useful Enemies: When Waging Wars is More Important than Winning Them*. New Haven: Yale University Press.

Keenan, Thomas P. (2014), *Technocreep: The Surrender of Privacy and the Capitalization of Intimacy*. Vancouver: Greystone Books.

Kidd, Benjamin (1898), *The Control of the Tropics*. London: Macmillan.

Kirkby, Diane and Coleborne, Catharine, eds. (2001), *Law, History, Colonialism: The Reach of Empire*. Manchester: Manchester University Press.

Kothari, Rita (2013), "Caste in a Casteless Language." *Economic and Political Weekly* 48: 7, 60–68.

Lazarus, Neil (2011), *The Postcolonial Unconscious*. Cambridge: Cambridge University Press.

Lenin, V. I. (1965) [1917], *Imperialism, The Highest Stage of Capitalism. A Popular Outline*. Peking: Foreign Languages Press.

Linklater, Andro (2014), *Owning the Earth: The Transforming History of Land Ownership*. London: Bloomsbury.

Lucas, C. P., ed. (1912), *Lord Durham's Report on the Affairs of British North America*, 3 vols. Oxford: Clarendon Press.

Luce, Edward (2014), "The Era of American Drone Supremacy is Fading." *Financial Times*, June 29.

Lugard, Frederick John D. (1922), *The Dual Mandate in British Tropical Africa*. Edinburgh: Blackwood.

Lynd, Robert Wilson (1911), "Preface on Nationalism and Nationality," in *Nationalities and Subject Races: Report of Conference held in Caxton Hall, Westminster, June 28-30, 1910*. London: P. S. King, vii–xii.

Mackridge, Peter (2009), *Language and National Identity in Greece*. New York: Oxford University Press.

Mamdani, Mahmood (2002), *When Victims Become Killers: Colonialism, Nativism, and the Genocide in Rwanda*. Princeton: Princeton University Press.

Marquard, Leo (1957), *South Africa's Colonial Policy*. Johannesburg: Institute of Race Relations.

Marx, Karl (1973), "The Eighteenth Brumaire of Louis Bonaparte," trans. Ben Fowkes, in *Surveys from Exile*, ed. David Fernback. London: Penguin, 143–249.

Marx, Karl and Engels, Friedrich (2002) [1848], *The Communist Manifesto*, trans. Samuel Moore. London: Penguin.

Mbembe, Achille (1990), "Pouvoir, violence at accumulation." *Politique Africaine* 39, 7–24.

Mbembe, Achille (1992a), "The Banality of Power and the Aesthetics of Vulgarity in the Postcolony." *Public Culture* 4: 2, 1–30.

Mbembe, Achille (1992b), "Provisional Notes on the Postcolony." *Africa* 62: 1, 3–37.

Mbembe, Achille (2001), *On the Postcolony*, trans. A. M. Berrett. Berkeley: University of California Press.

Mbembe, Achille (2003), "Necropolitics," trans. Libby Meintjes. *Public Culture* 15: 1, 11–40.

Mbembe, Achille (2010), *Sortir de la grande nuit. Essai sur l'Afrique décolonisée*. Paris: La Découverte.

McClintock, Anne (1995), *Imperial Leather: Race, Gender and Sexuality in the Colonial Context*. New York: Routledge.

Memmi, Albert (1967) [1957], *The Colonizer and the Colonized*. Boston: Beacon Press.

Meredith, David and Havinden, Michael A. (2002), *Colonialism and Development: Britain and Its Tropical Colonies, 1850-1960*. London: Routledge.

Merle, Marcel (1969), *L'Anticolonialisme européen, de Las Casas à Marx*. Paris: Colin.

Mishra, Pankaj (2012), *From the Ruins of Empire: The Revolt against the West and the Remaking of Asia.* London: Allen Lane.

Mitchell, Timothy (2002), *Rule of Experts: Egypt, Techno-Politics, Modernity.* Berkeley: University of California Press.

Moses, A. Dirk, ed. (2008), *Empire, Colony, Genocide: Conquest, Occupation, and Subaltern Resistance in World History.* New York: Berghahn.

Moses, A. Dirk (2011), "Hannah Arendt, Imperialisms, and the Holocaust," in Volker Langbehn and Mohammad Salama, eds., *German Colonialism: Race, the Holocaust and Postwar Germany.* New York: Columbia University Press, 72–92.

Motyl, Alexander J. (2001), *Imperial Ends: The Decay, Collapse and Revival of Empires.* New York: Columbia University Press.

Moyn, Samuel (2010), *The Last Utopia: Human Rights in History.* Cambridge, MA: Harvard University Press.

Mrazek, Rudolf (2002), *Engineers of Happy Land: Technology and Nationalism in a Colony.* Princeton: Princeton University Press.

Naipaul, V. S. (1961), *A House for Mr Biswas.* London: Deutsch.

Naipaul, V. S. (1967), *The Mimic Men.* London: Deutsch.

Nandy, Ashis (1983), *The Intimate Enemy: Loss and Recovery of Self under Colonialism.* Delhi: Oxford University Press.

Ngũgĩ, Wa Thiong'o (1981), *Decolonizing the Mind.* London: James Currey.

Nixon, Rob (2011), *Slow Violence and the Environmentalism of the Poor.* Cambridge, MA: Harvard University Press.

Nkrumah, Kwame (1965), *Neo-Colonialism: The Last Stage of Imperialism.* London: Heinemann.

O'Callaghan, Sean (2001), *To Hell or Barbados: The Ethnic Cleansing of Ireland.* Dingle: Brandon Books.

O'Gorman, Eleanor (2011), *The Front Line Runs through Every Woman: Women and Local Resistance in the Zimbabwean Liberation War.* Woodbridge: James Currey.

Omissi, D. E. (1990), *Air Power and Colonial Control: The Royal Air Force, 1919–1939.* Manchester: Manchester University Press.

Ophir, Adi, Givoni, Michal, and Ḥanafī, Sārī (2009), *The Power of Inclusive Exclusion: Anatomy of Israeli Rule in the Occupied Palestinian Territories.* New York: Zone Press.

Ortiz, Fernando (1995) [1941], *Cuban Counterpoint: Tobacco and Sugar*, trans. Harriet de Onís. Durham, NC: Duke University Press.

Osterhammel, Jürgen (1997) [1995], *Colonialism: A Theoretical Overview*, trans. Shelley L. Frisch. Princeton: Marcus Wiener.

Osterhammel, Jürgen and Petersson, Niels P. (2009), *Globalization: A Short History*. Princeton: Princeton University Press.

Petersson, Frederik (2013), *Willi Münzenberg, The League Against Imperialism and the Comintern, 1925–1933*, 2 vols. New York: Edward Mellen Press.

Pietsch, Tamson (2013), *Empire of Scholars: Universities, Networks and the British Academic World, 1850–1939*. Manchester: Manchester University Press.

Porter, Bernard (1968), *Critics of Empire: British Radical Attitudes to Colonialism in Africa 1895–1914*. London: Macmillan; New York: St Martin's Press.

Pratt, Mary Louise (1994), "Transculturation and Autoethnography: Peru 1615/1980," in Francis Barker, Peter Hulme, and Margaret Iverson, eds., *Colonial Discourse/Postcolonial Theory*. Manchester: Manchester University Press, 24–46.

Rancière, Jacques (2004) [1983], *The Philosopher and His Poor*, trans. John Drury, Corinne Oster, and Andrew Parker. Durham, NC: Duke University Press.

Robbins, Bruce (2012), *Perpetual War: Cosmopolitanism from the Viewpoint of Violence*. Durham, NC: Duke University Press.

Rodinson, Maxime (1973), *Israel: A Colonial-Settler State?* New York: Monad Press.

Rodriguez, Ileana, ed. (2001), *The Latin American Subaltern Studies Reader*. Durham, NC: Duke University Press.

Saada, Emmanuelle (2012), *Empire's Children: Race, Filiation and Citizenship in the French Colonies*, trans. Arthur Goldhammer. Chicago: University of Chicago Press.

Said, Edward W. (1978), *Orientalism: Western Representations of the Orient*. London: Routledge and Kegan Paul.

Said, Edward W. (1993), *Culture and Imperialism*. London: Chatto and Windus.

Said, Edward W. (1994), *Representations of the Intellectual: The 1993 Reith Lectures*. London: Vintage.

Sangari, Kumkum and Vaid, Sudesh (1989), *Recasting Women: Essays in Colonial History*. New Delhi: Kali for Women.

Sartre, Jean-Paul (2001), *Colonialism and Neo-colonialism*, trans. Azzedine Haddour, Steve Brewer, and Terry McWilliams. London: Routledge.

Schmitt, Carl (2003) [1950], *The Nomos of the Earth in the International Law of the Jus Publicum Europaeum*, trans. G. L. Ulmen. New York: Telos Press.

Scott, James C. (1985), *Weapons of the Weak: Everyday Forms of Peasant Resistance*. New Haven: Yale University Press.

Scott, James C. (1990), *Domination and the Arts of Resistance: Hidden Transcripts*. New Haven: Yale University Press.

Scott, James C. (1998), *Seeing Like a State: How Certain Schemes to Improve the Human Condition Have Failed*. New Haven: Yale University Press.

Seeley, John Robert (1971) [1883], *The Expansion of England*, ed. John Gross. Chicago: University of Chicago Press.

Shehadeh, Raja (1985), *Occupier's Law: Israel and the West Bank*. Washington, DC: Institute for Palestinian Studies.

Sherwood, Marika (2007), *After Abolition: Britain and the Slave Trade since 1807*. London: I. B. Tauris.

Silverstein, Adam J. (2010), *Islamic History: A Very Short Introduction*. Oxford: Oxford University Press.

Singh, Bhagat (1933) [1923], "The Problem of Punjab's Language and Script." http://.en.wikisource.org/wiki/The_Problem_of_Punjab%E2%80%99s_Language_and_Script.

Singh, Harleen (2014), *The Rani of Jhansi: Gender, History, and Fable in India*. Cambridge: Cambridge University Press.

Slaughter, Joseph R. (2007), *Human Rights, Inc.: The World Novel, Narrative Form, and International Law*. New York: Fordham University Press.

Smith, Linda Tuhiwai (1998), *Decolonising Methodologies*. London: Zed Books.

Smith, Zadie (2000), *White Teeth*. London: Hamish Hamilton.

Spivak, Gayatri Chakravorty (1988), "Can the Subaltern Speak? Speculations on Widow Sacrifice," in *Marxism and the Interpretation of Culture*, ed. Cary Nelson and Lawrence Grossberg. London: Macmillan, 271–313.

Spivak, Gayatri Chakravorty (2003), *Death of a Discipline*. New York: Columbia University Press.

Springhall, John (2001), *Decolonization since 1945: The Collapse of European Overseas Empires*. Basingstoke: Palgrave Macmillan.

St Clair, William (1972), *That Greece Might Still Be Free: The Philhellenes in the War of Independence*. Oxford: Oxford University Pres.

Stallybrass, Peter and White, Alan (1986), *The Politics and Poetics of Transgression*. London: Routledge.

Stannard, David E. (1992), *American Holocaust: Columbus and the Conquest of the New World*. New York: Oxford University Press.

Stiglitz, Joseph (2002), *Globalization and Its Discontents*. London: Allen Lane.

Stokes, Eric (1959), *The English Utilitarians and India*. Oxford: Clarendon Press.

Stoler, Laura Ann (1995), *Race and the Education of Desire: Foucault's History of Sexuality and the Colonial Order of Things*. Durham, NC: Duke University Press.

Tett, Gillian (2010), *Fool's Gold: How Unrestrained Greed Corrupted a Dream, Shattered Global Markets and Unleashed a Catastrophe*, 2nd ed. London: Abacus.

Thomas, Nicholas (1994), *Colonialism's Culture: Anthropology, Travel and Government*. Princeton: Princeton University Press.

Thoreau, Henry David (2008), *Walden, Civil Disobedience, and Other Writings*, 3rd ed., ed. William Rossi. New York: Norton.

Tsao, Roy T. (2002), "The Three Phases of Arendt's Theory of Totalitarianism." *Social Research* 69: 2, 579–619.

UNESCO (1969) [1961], *The Race Question in Modern Science: Race and Science*. New York: Columbia University Press.

Veracini, Lorenzo (2006), *Israel and Settler Society*. London: Pluto Press.

Veracini, Lorenzo (2010), *Settler Colonialism: A Theoretical Overview*. Basingstoke: Palgrave Macmillan.

Wakefield, E. B. (1849), *A View of the Art of Colonisation*. London: John W. Parker.

Wallerstein, Immanuel (2004), *World Systems Analysis: An Introduction*. Durham, NC: Duke University Press.

Watt, Douglas (2007), *The Price of Scotland: Darien, Union and the Wealth of Nations*. Edinburgh: Luath Press.

Weil, Simone (2003), *Simone Weil on Colonialism: An Ethic of the Other*, trans. J. P. Little. Lanham, MD: Rowman and Littlefield.

Woollacott, Angela (2001), *To Try Her Fortune in London: Australian Women, Colonialism, and Modernity*. Oxford: Oxford University Press.

Young, Robert J. C. (1995), *Colonial Desire: Hybridity in Culture, Theory and Race*. London: Routledge.

Young, Robert J. C. (2001), *Postcolonialism: An Historical Introduction*. Oxford: Blackwell.

Young, Robert J. C. (2003), *Postcolonialism: A Very Short Introduction*. Oxford: Oxford University Press

Young, Robert J. C. (2004) [1990], *White Mythologies: Writing History and the West*, 2nd ed. London: Routledge.

Young, Robert J. C. (2005a), "Postcolonialism: From Bandung to the Tricontinental," *historein/ιστορειν* 5: 11–21. http://www.nnet.gr/historein/historeinfiles/histvolumes/hist05/historein5--young.pdf.

Young, Robert J. C. (2005b) "Fanon and the Turn to Armed Struggle in Africa." *Wasafiri* 44, 33–41.

Young, Robert J. C. (2006), "Gilberto Freyre and the Lusotropical Atlantic." *Unisa Latin American Report* 22: 1–2, 5–21.

Young, Robert J. C. (2008) *The Idea of English Ethnicity*. Oxford: Blackwell.

Young, Robert J. C. (2011), "International Anti-Colonialism: The Fenian Invasions of Canada," in *Studies in Settler Colonialism: Politics, Identity and Culture*, ed. Fiona Bateman and Lionel Pilkington. Basingstoke: Palgrave Macmillan, 75–89.

Young, Robert J. C. (2012), "Postcolonial Remains." *New Literary History* 43: 1, 19–42.

Young-Bruehl, Elisabeth (2004) [1977], *Hannah Arendt: For Love of the World*, 2nd ed. New Haven: Yale University Press.

Name Index

Empire, Colony, Postcolony, First Edition. Robert J. C. Young.
© 2015 Robert J. C. Young. Published 2015 by John Wiley & Sons, Ltd.

Subject Index

Empire, Colony, Postcolony, First Edition. Robert J. C. Young.
© 2015 Robert J. C. Young. Published 2015 by John Wiley & Sons, Ltd.